Lisa Fitzpatrick

Enjoying
Style
& Fashion

with Tara King

BLACKWATER PRESS

Blackwater Press Ltd.

1–5 North Frederick Street, Dublin 1

jloconnor@eircom.net

© Lisa Fitzpatrick, 2010

Edited by: Claire Rourke, Bookends Publishing

Design, layout and cover: Niamh Carey

ISBN 978-0-9563541-7-4

The author and publisher gratefully acknowledge the following for permission to reproduce photographs:

Mark Doyle Photographs, Robert Doyle, Tara King, Barry McCall, Muiris Moynihan, Theresa Murray, Ross Nugent, Rikard Österlund , John Ryan and Uzoma

Dreamstime, Getty Images, iStockphoto.com

Contents

Acknowledgements

To my mum, I love you so much, you're my heart and soul, you have taught me to be the mother I am.

To my publisher, John O'Connor, a huge thank you from my heart for making my dream a reality, you are such a gentleman, to you and your beautiful wife, Laserina. Thank you.

I would like to thank Tara King for her hard work and assistance throughout this journey. Great getting to know you.

Noel Kelly, NK Management, my pal, your 'can do' attitude is infectious. Thanks for all your advise, support and friendship.

Niamh, NK Management, my very stylish friend, thank you for being you. I love our endless chats and your professionalism.

A big thank you to my editor Claire Rourke, and designers Niamh Carey and Liz White for all your work, support and for sharing your knowledge.

Fiona Fitzpatrick, you are my sounding board and a true friend.

A big thank you to Lexus for helping me get from interview to interview in the most elegant and stylish way possible.

To the contributors, I cannot thank you all enough for offering up your time and for sharing with me your vast expertise and knowledge: Barry McCall, Caprice, Dr Rosemary Coleman, Dominic Munnelly, Emma O'Connor Sunglasses Hut in Dundrum Town Centre, Erin O'Connor, Gary Kavanagh, Jackie O'Reilly of Optical Express in Dundrum Town Centre, Jen Kelly, Karen Millen, Kate Coughlan, Louis Copeland, Mary Mullins, Mark O'Keeffe, Nina Divito, Paula Callan O'Keeffe, Paul Costelloe, Rachel Kavanagh, Richard Lewis, Tara Fay and Tina Leonard.

Over the years I have dealt with many people in the media, I would like to take this opportunity to thank them sincerely for all their support and kindness, support and airbrushing.

VIP 2007, this started the journey. Thank you.

To all my family and friends, you have all supported me in many different ways, you know who you are. This has been a very exciting journey that would not have happened without you.

xXx

Dedication

I dedicate this book to the three most special people in my life.

Paul – my husband and best friend – and our wonderful children
Sophie and Dalton who never fail to make my day so much brighter!
You have been with me every step of the way and I love you all so very much. xx

Introduction

On the day I was born, Rod Stewart's 'You Wear It Well' was number one in the charts. Some might call it coincidence, I prefer to think of it as fate – or at least a clue as to what lay ahead!

Ladies, I was once a size eighteen and I know the various difficulties that accompany the battle against fluctuating weight. This is precisely why I detest those articles that group women into categories such as pear shape and apple shape. The way I see it, every woman's body is completely different and cannot be categorised under any one label.

Similarly, you often hear the phrase, 'Style is not something you have, it's something you inherit.' NONSENSE! Anyone can be stylish if they want to be and, when you think about it, everyone is stylish in their own, individual way.

As you make your way through my book, you will notice a major emphasis on positive thinking and the wonderfully powerful impact it can have on your life. My reason for including this in the book is quite simple – I have always believed that the best makeovers begin from within. Believe me, no amount of make-up or hair styling will make you feel your best if your esteem and confidence are rock bottom.

When I set about writing this book, I knew from the start that it was never going to be about style and style alone. I wanted to incorporate all aspects, from style improvement and skincare to outlook and attitude. I certainly don't claim to know everything – I am still learning every day. I do hope, however, that this book will be the first of many because I feel as though I'm still growing as a person and still absorbing new information. This time next year, I know I will have so many more experiences to share with you and even more advice to offer.

So take this book for what it was intended … a little gift from me to help make your life bigger, better and brighter.

Enjoy the book and don't forget to check out my website (www.fitzpatrickstyle.com) and follow Lisa Fitzpatrick Style on Facebook!

Lisa Fitzpatrick xXx

I don't look like this all the time! Hours of preparation are involved, which goes to show you it can be done!

Confidence
Positivity
Posture
Smile!

Take Action in Your Life

> *"Nobody can make you feel inferior without your permission."*
>
> Eleanor Roosevelt

When you have kids, you become an authority on all things cartoon related, in particular Disney characters.

Pocahontas, Mickey Mouse, Cruella De Vil, I'm on first name terms with them all. What I particularly love, however, are the words of wisdom that came from the great mind of the man who created them, Walt Disney.

His words have long been used to motivate people from all walks of life, from businessmen and CEOs to teenagers and college students.

One of Mr Disney's inspiring quotations is: "The only way to get started is to quit talking and begin doing." This has always been my motto in life and, girls, let me tell you, it has worked for me. Being proactive is the only sure way of achieving your dreams. Treat this as your wake-up call, change your attitude and decide now what you want from your life.

Lisa Fitzpatrick

THE LIST

"A good goal should scare you a little, and excite you a lot!"

Joe Vitale

When you have decided what it is you want, go out and get it — stop dreaming about it! Make it happen. Better still, make it happen, now.

The best way to do this is to start with a list.

The more specific you are, the better chance you have of achieving what you write down. At first, set goals that are realistic and obtainable then, as you progress, begin setting higher goals. I have always been of the firm belief that anyone who is serious about progressing in life should have a list of goals they want to accomplish. Forget the New Year's resolutions nonsense! Self-improvement should not start on 1 January, nor should a diet only ever start on a Monday. Your goals should provide you with a clear purpose but, most importantly, they should encourage you to become more proactive. Just imagine how happy you will be when you reach the coveted finish line, so don't be afraid to set yourself high goals.

GO FOR IT!

"After all these years, I am still involved in the process of self-discovery. It's better to explore life and make mistakes than to play it safe. Mistakes are part of the dues one pays for a full life."

Sophia Loren

It's all too easy to sit back and blame someone else for your situation but only you are responsible for the choices you make in your life. Accept responsibility for your decisions and concentrate on ways in which you can improve your life. We've all made choices we regret, but the worst thing you can do is dwell on those mistakes. After all, when you made your choice, you did so because you felt it was the right thing to do at the time. In my experience, it's the things you don't do that will cause you the most regret in later years.

I often hear people say, 'I'd love to write a book.' So go write it! I've often thought about it, but now I'm turning that dream into a reality. You have to understand that your dream will not stand a chance of becoming a reality unless you get the ball moving. Yes, it's terrifying and nerve-wracking but anything worth fighting for is not going to be stress free. It's all too easy to fear the idea of moving on to bigger and better things. Fortunately, however, the solution is rather simple. Don't be afraid ... be excited!

NOTHING STOPPING YOU!

"Even from a very early age, I knew I didn't want to miss out on anything life had to offer just because it might be considered dangerous."

Nicole Kidman

Regardless of whether or not you like your job, only you can make the decision to be the best that you can be in your chosen occupation.

There's absolutely nothing stopping you from walking into your job every day and being the person who looks on at others acquiring better salaries, better promotions or moving on to better jobs. Similarly, there's nothing stopping you from being part of that success group.

Begin by visualising yourself as the person climbing the ladder and try to picture the end result. Now, jot down what you will have to do in order to achieve the end result.

Maybe you have always wanted to learn how to play an instrument or perhaps you have always envisioned yourself designing clothes. Everyone's dream is different. No matter how crazy yours might seem, whether you want to become a doctor or a parachute instructor, it still deserves a place on your goal list.

Look in the local newspaper or on the internet to find the nearest course that will help you on your way towards achieving your dream. I have always placed great faith in the law of attraction and how people can encourage many wonderful things into their lives by visualising them. Believe firmly that your goals will materialise. If it helps, create a vision board for yourself. Whether it's a particular type of car or house that you want to own some day, stick a picture of it up on the board and keep it there as a form of encouragement and motivation.

Throughout this book, there are so many stories from people who dared to chase their dream. As I interviewed each person, I couldn't help but notice that the one thing they all shared was an unwavering belief in their ability to make their dreams a reality. Their optimism was infectious, while their work ethic was more than amazing. They are the kind of people who leave you feeling inspired and motivated. Having someone to look up to, whether they are famous or otherwise, can be extremely beneficial. Think of a person who is currently living their dream. What did they do to get there? Are they optimistic by nature? Are they good negotiators? Are they clear concise speakers? Do they invest long hours? Do they surround themselves with positive influences? Are they risk takers? What is it that people admire about them? Learn from their behaviour and use that knowledge to improve your own character.

The one thing you will more than likely notice about the person you choose is their habit of grabbing every opportunity that crosses their path. If you want to get the most out of your life, you too will need to develop this trait. For instance, if there is an interview for a better job or a better position in the company your currently work in, don't be one bit afraid to go for it. On that note, it's important that you don't fear being rejected either.

"The big secret in life is that there is no big secret. Whatever your goal, you can get there if you're willing to work."

Oprah Winfrey

Changing your outlook and how you feel about yourself may be difficult at the beginning. It's all about breaking those old habits you have acquired over the years and encouraging your body and mind to follow a new and more beneficial routine.

Don't allow yourself to feel overwhelmed by it all. Instead, just concentrate on your:

Confidence

Positivity

Posture

Smile!

"The most courageous act is still to think for yourself. Aloud." Coco Chanel

These are wonderful tools that every person should have in abundance. When you have attained them, you are halfway to anywhere you want to be.

Look at Richard Branson, for example. He is always using these four basic principals and they certainly haven't done him any harm! His confidence appears to be unshakeable as he takes on greater and more extravagant challenges without any fear of criticism or failure. Likewise his positivity has been pivotal to his success. From the very beginning, he had people telling him he couldn't succeed, yet here he is today standing tall as one of the most successful businessmen in the world. Lastly, can you even visualise him sulking or complaining? Probably not, because he always has such a bright smile on his face.

Richard Branson

Confidence

"While clothes may not make the woman, they certainly have a strong effect on her self-confidence – which, I believe, does make the woman."

Mary Kaye Ashe

We all know of someone whose very presence can light up a room. They appear genuinely happy and almost immune to any negativity. Believe it or not, the only difference between you and them is confidence.

Before I go any further, I should point out there is a big difference between being confident and being cocky. Be careful you don't tread the boards of the latter.

Years ago, self-confidence was something I didn't possess. This was mostly because I hadn't been to college and, for a long time, I didn't feel very educated. Then I realised that I possessed something many college graduates didn't – I was streetwise. I come from a manufacturing, retail and wholesale background, so I could pretty much buy and sell you anything!

Lisa Fitzpatrick, Style Seminar at *Xposé Live*.

While I do think a degree is important for a lot of careers, I eventually realised that it didn't matter that I didn't have a college education. I had worked extremely hard and, with a little bit of luck thrown in along the way, I still managed to be successful without the input of college. I admire anyone who decides to educate themselves further whatever way they choose to go about it, but the college route just wasn't for me.

I think it's fundamental for kids to understand the importance of work as well as education. I remember having had all kinds of jobs as a teenager, from working in Bewleys to packing grocery bags. Each and every one of these experiences was important in its own way because each experience taught me something new.

No one has to be perfect all of the time. In fact, no one has to be perfect ever! All you have to do is make the effort and you will feel so much better as a result – things like making time to enjoy a date night with your husband, remembering your friends' birthdays, emailing people nice gestures, sending someone a text out of the blue. When you make the effort, all these nice positive things will come back to you.

I fully believe that if you can help someone in some way or give them your support, karma will come full circle and your positivity will be returned. I love supporting and helping people because I love to see them grow as individuals. It's great to see someone striving for something and if I can help them in any way possible, I am more than happy to do so.

Envy is not an emotion I befriend.

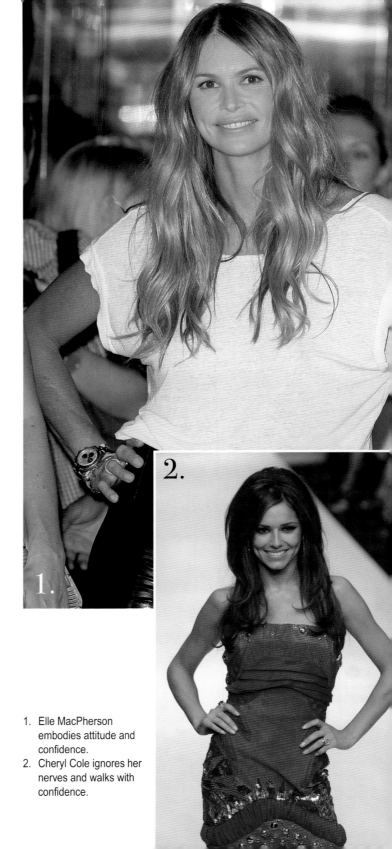

1. Elle MacPherson embodies attitude and confidence.
2. Cheryl Cole ignores her nerves and walks with confidence.

Positivity

"Delete the negative, accentuate the positive!"

Donna Karan

I often notice that some people have the mentality whereby if something bad happens during their day, they dwell on it continuously.

It's often the case that when one negative incident occurs, things get progressively worse as the day goes on – to the point that our focus is always on the bad things that have happened.

But we can change this through thinking positively. If something bad happens to me, I never allow it to take over my day and absorb my energy. If I were to dent the side of my car at 8 o'clock in the morning, I wouldn't talk about it continuously nor would I allow any annoyance or frustration to fester inside me. Talking about an incident and replaying it in my head would drive me nuts.

I'm the kind of person who puts a negative experience behind me and gets on with things. I just won't allow it to hold me back. But this didn't come naturally, it is actually something I try really hard to do and it's a skill that you too can teach yourself. Even if you have been pessimistic by nature, if you practise being positive, you will come to see that it's so much nicer to have an open, optimistic attitude rather than a negative, despondent outlook.

Donna Karan

Some years ago, I completed a course on positive thinking with Tony Robbins and I can still remember the profound impact it had on me. It definitely made me realise that I could achieve whatever I dreamed of and that anything really was possible. Today, there are very few things that I will allow to impact negatively on my mood. For instance, I never allow people to get me down. I don't need to be liked and loved by everyone because I know I'm already loved by the most important people in my life – the people that I care about and the people that I work with.

Focus more on what you have and not what others have.

You may look at someone else and think they have it all, but when it comes down to it, you don't know what goes on behind closed doors. I remember years ago there was one particular woman who, in my eyes, had the perfect life. It was only when she shared with me some details about her life that I realised she was very good at faking the good life. She had her own traumas to deal with. We all have our issues, you just need to acquire the strength to deal with them and move on.

Part of the 'moving on' process involves learning how to take things with a pinch of salt. When you look at magazines, remember the pictures are airbrushed. Even Cindy Crawford once admitted that she doesn't wake up looking like the Cindy Crawford we see in magazines. Celebrities may appear as though they have the perfect life but always remember they have their own problems too.

Train yourself to automatically see the positive aspects of challenges and obstacles. Look beyond the problem and see what benefits it might bring. Will it make you a better person in the long run? Perhaps it will make you stronger. If you find the daily news is becoming more and more depressing, then don't listen to it. It's all about rewiring your brain and training yourself to see immediately the positive rather than the negative.

To help you on your way, try to surround yourself only with successful, positive people. This is vital when it comes to achieving success. Cut back on contact with people you consider to be draining or a negative influence. They will only yearn to see you fail whereas successful people will encourage you to climb high.

I have a small number of people in my life who are my sounding boards. They each have very different lives but they're all wonderfully positive influences in their own individual ways. They are the kind of people who leave me feeling motivated and ready to battle against any challenge. They reinforce my faith in my own abilities and reassure me when I need it most. However in order to have these kind of people in your life, you need to be that kind of person to your friends. Ask yourself honestly, do you listen to your friends' problems? Do you encourage them to follow their dreams? Do you even know what their true dreams are?

Positive thinking will come so much more easily if you have a good attitude towards heath and fitness. Think about it. If you only ever eat junk food, then how can you expect to be feeling anything other than incredibly lethargic and run down? Fruit and vegetables on the other hand are full of minerals and vitamins and will serve your body a better deal in the long run.

I eat well from Monday to Friday but, by the weekend, forget it! I eat what I want, when I want. The advantage to this is that when you allow yourself time off for treats, you tend not to overindulge. I know a lot of people on diets who find themselves constantly thinking about the foods they can't have. This is because they deny themselves these 'treat' foods and, as such, crave what they can't have. Know your limits and don't ban anything completely from your diet.

Whether your goal is to eat healthily or lose weight, expect temptation to make an appearance at some stage. If you find that you don't have the willpower to resist it, don't beat yourself up about it. As I said earlier, I try to eat healthily midweek, but sometimes I give in. I just try my best and that's all I can ask of myself.

"If you do a little research, it is going to become very evident that anyone who ever accomplished anything did not know how they were going to do it, they just knew they were going to do it."

Bob Proctor

I often think back to when I was a bigger size. I seemed to grow and grow without even realising. Suddenly I was a size eighteen and weighed fourteen stone. I remember I became very adept at dressing around my weight so that no one would figure out my true size.

A defining moment for me came when I was walking through the security checkpoint in Dublin airport. I was wearing a beautiful suit, however, because of my weight I couldn't button up the trousers at the back. Fortunately, the jacket was long enough to cover it up. As long as I kept the jacket on, no one would know any different. At the time, I was on a business trip which included many well-known figures, all of whom were in the queue directly behind me. You can therefore envisage the look of horror that shot across my face when the security guard suddenly asked me to remove my coat and bags. Bear in mind, it wasn't unusual for me to leave my jacket on in a restaurant and endure unbearable heat rather than take it off and reveal the full extent of my weight gain, so you can imagine how unwilling I was to remove my jacket on this particular occasion.

My attempt was met with yet another response about it being airport security policy that all jackets and bags be removed. I was out of options and out of luck. Removing my jacket, I kept looking straight ahead, refusing to think about what the people behind me might be saying about my unclosed buttons. Once I was finished at the security desk, I walked away with my head held high and promptly made for the ladies room where I locked myself in a cubicle and cried my eyes out. Within minutes, I was on the phone to my mum. After consoling me, her solution was that of every Irish mother. "Lisa get yourself a cup of tea and a muffin and you'll be fine!" Even looking back now, I just think, Oh those bloody muffins, that's why I found it so hard to lose weight!

It reached a point where I found it incredibly difficult to get nice clothes to fit my shape and, as a result, I would overcompensate by buying nice earrings, bags and shoes. I had box loads of shoes! One day, while I was showing a friend yet another pair of beautiful shoes I had bought, she just looked at me and very honestly said, 'Have you not got enough pairs of shoes and bags already? Would you not ever think of just losing weight?' I thought it was a bit harsh at the time, but I soon came to realise she was absolutely right.

When I gave birth to my daughter Sophie, I quickly realised that my weight would not provide me with the energy I needed to do simple things like play with her in the park. I didn't want to be the mum that sat on the bench, too tired to run around. I wanted to be out there playing with my daughter, I wanted to dress well and I wanted to feel good about myself. It took me three years, but I got there. To help me on my way, I got myself a personal trainer, Dominic Munnelly, who devised a personal diet and exercise plan for me. I wasn't expecting overnight results and I think that stood to me in the long term because it meant I didn't give up as easily especially during those difficult times when I felt I wasn't making any progress with my weight loss. I just knew that after years of putting on weight, it would take more than a seven-day wonder diet to shift it all.

When I interviewed the supermodel and businesswoman Caprice for this book, one of the things she said to me was, "Sugar is death – stay away from anything that contains sugar."

That, to me, is one piece of advice worth heeding. Set yourself a challenge of going a week without drinking anything fizzy and, by the seventh day, you should start to feel a nice difference in your energy levels. It goes without saying that you should also try to drink more water than caffeine. Most of us tend to reach for the sugar-fix when we're looking for a quick snack. Personally, I find it so much more effective to eat small healthy portions every three hours. That way I rarely find myself in a position where I'm craving a sugar rush.

Another idea is to eat before going to the supermarket. Have something small like a bowl of soup before you go because, as we all know only too well, if we shop on an empty stomach, we will more than likely return home with a trolley full of rubbish. Similarly, if you are going to a function at night, have your dinner or a light meal before heading out so that you don't overindulge when you get there.

Another good tip is to avoid eating after seven o'clock – as this helps you sleep better.

If ever you find yourself wondering whether or not a new diet craze genuinely works, then ask yourself this, "Does it make you move and pump a sweat? If it doesn't then how can it make you tone up or lose weight?"

People look at the magazines and see pictures of celebrities with amazing bodies accompanied by a headline like 'The New Diet That Really Works'. Let me tell you, these people only acquire their 'amazing bodies' though consistent and intensive workouts. It's no accident that they are in great shape and it's certainly not the result of any fad crash diet. They put in the work through a healthy diet and exercise and, from this, they enjoy the results. They are doing all the things that most people don't want to do. A lot of people never make it beyond the beginner stages of their health plan because they are not consistent and they question too much. They are experts on all the minor details like how many calories are in every spoonful and which carbohydrates they should be leaving out of their diet, yet when it comes down to the hard work of exercising, they fall back.

"Twenty years from now, you will be more disappointed by the things you didn't do than the things you did. So throw off the bowlines, sail away from the safe harbour, and catch the trade wins in your sails. Explore. Dream. Discover."

Mark Twain

21

So, ladies, do yourselves a favour and forget the diet fads. When it comes to losing weight and getting fit, a healthy diet and a thorough exercise routine are the only solutions that will work.

This brings me nicely to my next point. Don't forget to allow some fresh air into your lungs.

There's more to positivity than affirmations; it's about your mental well being in its entirety. I personally love going for a long walk or a bicycle ride as these are the kind of activities that rejuvenate my body, both mentally and physically. There's no denying that it's difficult to find time. Whether you're preparing lunches for the kids, making dinner, getting the groceries or just carrying out general day-to-day tasks, the constant go go go can be overwhelming. This is precisely why it is so important to allow yourself some down time. The more you look after yourself, the better you will feel.

Posture

Posture is something I became very conscious of back when my weight was much heavier. Whenever I sat into a chair, my thighs would look huge, whereas if I sat on the edge of a chair and crossed my legs, they would look half the size. To look at the camera face on, I appeared so much bigger, yet when I turned to the side, I would look nowhere near as big. I started to learn all the tips of the trade as time went on and, as you will see throughout this book, there are many tips out there to help you. I have experienced everything in this book first hand; I have gone through the tears, the drama and the many heartaches.

One of the many lessons experience has taught me is that body language is a powerful tool. In fact, I would advise anyone to sit in a restaurant with a cup of coffee and observe the body language of others. You will notice that a lot of people hunch their shoulders and don't carry themselves confidently. When I was bigger, I always hunched my shoulders. Looking back, I was carrying the weight of the world on them. When I became more confident, however, I trained myself to sit straight.

It's sometimes difficult, particularly when you're not used to it, but the good news is that there are techniques you can employ to help you on your way. For instance, when you sit down, put your bum in to the back

"I'm a giraffe. I even walk like a giraffe with a long neck and legs. It's a pretty dumb animal, mind you."

Sophia Loren

Keep those shoulders back.

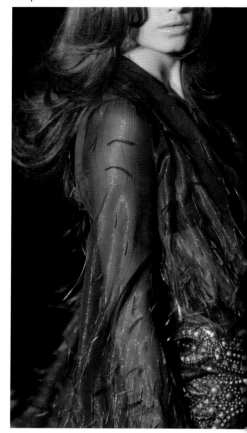

of the chair and sit upright. You don't have to sit straight all the time because, let's face it, no one can be that proper 100 per cent of the time – just try to do your best. I assure you when I'm at home, I relax across the sofa with my feet up and the last thing on my mind is my posture and how I'm sitting!

Smile

When you walk into a room, the best thing you can offer is a smile. There is nothing more attractive than someone who is welcoming, open, and possesses good posture and confidence. It has nothing to do with possessing the beautiful looks of a movie star, it's about having the right attitude. It's also about accepting yourself and being genuinely happy in your own skin.

Without make-up, I am white and freckly, however, I know exactly what shades of make-up suit me and, more importantly, I know how to apply them. This is because I made a point of learning the techniques though my friends in the Dublin hair and make-up salon, Brown Sugar.

We can all make ourselves look and feel good with the right tricks.

If you're self-conscious about any particular part of your body, don't give it your undivided attention – work your good assets instead. We all have those parts of ourselves that we don't like. Some of the most beautiful actresses in the world have their hang ups, but you would never notice their flaws because they don't dwell on them, they make the most of their best features.

If people always compliment you on your eyes, then apply the smokey eye shadow and make them stand out even more. If you have nice legs, put on a light shimmer tan and show them off. It really is all about emphasising your good areas.

And to conclude …

Worry less about what people think of you. When you start liking yourself, you open yourself up to others liking you. Don't be worried about how you will look at the wedding, the Communion or the fortieth birthday celebration, because you'll look fine! How do I know? Because your confidence, positivity, posture and smile will get you everywhere.

"People seldom notice old clothes if you wear a big smile."

Lee Mildon

When you look at this photo of Julia Roberts, what's the first thing you notice? Her make-up or her smile?

Styling Your Shape

Style Tips from the Icons

"Just around the corner in every woman's mind is a lovely dress, a wonderful suit, or an entire costume which will make an enchanting new creature of her."

Wilfelia Cushman

We all want to invest our hard-earned money in items that will last us a lifetime; items that will take us to any occasion and that will continue look in style years after we've bought them. Unfortunately, most of us end up spending our money on clothes that barely survive a few months. What woman hasn't at some stage cursed the beautiful clothes that failed to give her their money's worth? Finding those classic wardrobe items that are beautiful enough to outshine any trend may seem like a daunting task. Fortunately, this need not be the case and I'm about to show you the various items that have survived all fashion fads and continue to look effortlessly stylish regardless of the season. In fact, they are still as classic today as they were all those decades ago when they were designed.

Ladies, if you want class, elegance and style, you only have to look to the women who gave it to us.

The icons

1. Grace Kelly
2. Heidi Klum
3. Jennifer Aniston
4. Brigitte Bardot

LITTLE WHITE DRESS

We've all heard the line about how every woman should own a little black dress, but, for me, the little white dress (LWD) also reigns high on the must-have list. Feminine and understated, you can accessorise it to create whatever classic look you wish. In fact, why not give a nod to the bygone era of Grace Kelly and pair your LWD with a shawl and elegant heels? If you find the colour white leaves your complexion looking drained, opt instead for a dress in a very light baby pink or blue.

1. Marylin Monroe
2. Princess Diana
3. Jackie Onassis
4. Eva Longoria

27

THE TRENCH COAT

When Catherine Zeta Jones began wearing elegant trench coats with high heels, a love for the classic wardrobe was reignited once again.

Today, macs are available in an abundance of patterns, such as floral and check, but if you're looking for one that defies trends, opt for a solid colour such as the traditional cream or sandy brown. For a sophisticated evening look, keep an eye out for elegant silk macs in deep luxurious colours, such as purple or crimson.

When macs were first made back in the 1800s, various problems arose, most notably, the material of the coat melting in hot weather! Fortunately, today's quality macs are much more durable and with proper care, should last years.

1. Catherine Zeta Jones
2. Jackie Onassis
3. Twiggy and Erin O'Connor

"I started in the men's business, so I always sort of have a touch of menswear in terms of where I'm going ... and I think one of the sexiest looks for women, instead of wearing a low cut thing, sometimes a sharp suit is more."

Ralph Lauren

THE SUIT

For showbusiness fans, 1966 was the year actors Halle Berry and David Schwimmer were born. For sports fans, it was the year England defeated Germany to win the World Cup final but, for fashion followers, 1966 epitomised only one thing – Yves Saint Laurent's creation of his ever-classic suit, 'Le Smoking', which without doubt empowered women and revolutionised fashion.

For me, there is nothing nicer than the feeling I get when wearing a beautiful, tailored suit. I feel so self-assured and ready for any challenge thrown at me. A good suit will immediately create an air of professionalism and give you a wonderful injection of confidence.

I think most women will agree with me when I say there is something very feminine about the suit particularly one that fits well and flatters the figure. The style that best exemplifies my point is the skirt suit as worn by Marilyn Monroe and Carrie Bradshaw. This design is ultra-feminine, yet it still maintains a sharp, professional edge. Remember, you don't always have to settle for the traditional suit. There are so many other styles on the market that are slightly more creative but every bit as professional. Waistcoats, ruffled blouses, pencil skirt suits, see what's out there and find what works for you!

1. Sarah Jessica Parker
2. Brigitte Bardot
3. Marilyn Monroe
4. Charlize Theron

THE LITTLE BLACK DRESS

A little black dress (LBD) is one of the most versatile items a woman can own. In fact, I know several women who invest in one or two good quality black dresses and then go on to create countless different looks with accessories and shoes. Each time they wear the dress, it looks like a completely different outfit.

Regardless of the event, the LBD can be adapted to the occasion. The trick is to invest time and thought into the kind of accessories you will wear with the dress. (For more advice on accessorising your LBD, see page 105.)

1. Grace Kelly
2. Kate Moss
3. Audrey Hepburn
4. Kate Winslet

THE WHITE SHIRT

Where on earth would we be without the faithful white shirt in our wardrobes? There are many styles that work brilliantly with a white shirt, but, in my opinion, the classic is the white shirt and blue jeans look. This look has defied all trends and yet still manages to best combine casual with sexy. Whether you choose to pair it with high-heeled boots or shoes, this outfit would work just as well for a day shopping as it would for a night out. Since I began my styling career, I always maintained it was worth investing in a good quality white shirt. In fact, the more tailored the look, the better.

On that note, don't ignore the white shirts with elegant details such as ruffles and belts which Marlene Dietrich demonstrates beautifully how both the plain and the detailed style of shirt can flatter the figure.

5.

1.

2.

3.

4.

1. Marlene Dietrich
2. Marlene Dietrich
3. Gwen Stefani
4. Kate Moss
5. Kate Hudson

"I have often said that I wish I had invented blue jeans: the most spectacular, the most practical, the most relaxed and nonchalant. They have expression, modesty, sex appeal, simplicity — all I hope for in my clothes."

Yves Saint Laurent

Gwyneth Paltrow

DENIM JEANS

At first, I was extremely wary of covering jeans in this book for the simple reason being that it's such an individual topic. In fact, it's only when you delve into the details of denim manufacturing that you begin to understand just how akin to a science it has become.

The more I thought about it, however, the more I began to realise that I couldn't write a fashion book without covering the one item that has been a staple fixture in every woman's wardrobe for decades.

As such, I decided to enlist the help of someone who could offer the best advice possible. Who better for the job than a denimologist?

Whether you want to create the illusion of a slim figure or a tall frame, I discovered to my delight that there's a style for every requirement.

- Bootcut jeans suit quite a lot of different figures. They are particularly good for balancing out your shape, unlike the skinny jean which will just make your body appear out of proportion if you don't have the figure for it.

- If you want to appear taller, buy jeans with a mid-to-high rise. A long, straight-leg jean is brilliant for creating the illusion of longer legs. You should also go for a dark-wash denim as this creates the illusion of a longer slimmer legs.

- Petite women often have trouble finding jeans, however, they will be pleased to hear that brands such as Pepe and Salsa have jeans with a thirty-inch leg.

- If you're having your jeans altered, make sure you ask the seamstress to reattach the hem afterwards. Sometimes jeans just don't look right if the hem is not visible.

- When it comes to sizing, you may find that you're a size ten in one brand and a size fourteen in another. This has a lot to do with the country from where the brand originates. For example, Italian and French brands are very small fitting whereas the US brands are slightly bigger. If you know where the brand is from, then you will know whether or not you need to go up or down a size when trying them on.

- When it comes to washing jeans, each pair will have their own specific instructions. To ensure the longevity of your jeans, it's absolutely vital that you always follow the washing instructions. To prevent the colour of your jeans from fading, make sure you turn them inside-out before washing. Do this when ironing as well.

- A number of different factors will determine the price of jeans. In fact, when it comes to jeans, you really do get what you pay for as the price usually reflects the amount of work that has been put in them.

When you walk into a denim shop, you will see a variety of beautiful blues, but in order to achieve the array of different denims, a long dyeing process is involved. In the dyeing factory, the workers are literally covered from head to toe in blue because they're constantly blending colours to get the right shade of blue. This is very time consuming which again, leads to a higher price tag. Other jeans may have Swarkovski crystal

Scarlett Johansson

embellishments or a lot of distressing detail and, again, this would all be reflected in the price. The price of some brands may appear excessive, but you're far better off buying one good pair of jeans instead of five poor-quality pairs. Jeans are a staple item of your everyday wardrobe and they're also an item that won't date, which is why it's good to invest in quality.

- When buying jeans, make sure you buy them as snug-fitting as possible. The more you wear the jeans, the more they will stretch, usually by about an inch and a half. Don't buy them too tight around the waistband, however, as this is the one part that will not stretch. You should notice that the material around the legs and bum area will have stretched after one or two wears.

- If you are pregnant, it's a good idea to invest in good-quality maternity jeans as you will more than likely continue wearing them in the months after you have given birth.

- There are so many new advances being made in the denim industry. For example, if you have some weight around the stomach region, then you should try the new tummy tuck jeans (Pamela Scott do a great pair). Also available are new Wonder Jeans. Thanks to the panels built into the back of the jeans, they hold and lift the bum for the length of time you're wearing them!

- There's the unwritten rule that you should never wear a denim top with denim jeans. For some women, however, this look actually works. It is ok to team a light, oversized denim shirt with a dark pair of jeans. Alexa Chung models this look all the time, however she's one of the lucky few who can get away with it.

- A common mistake women make when shopping for jeans is that not having the patience to try on various styles, often they don't bring along the proper shoes to try on with them either.

- When shopping for jeans, you should know what suits your figure. For example, if you have a little bit of weight around your midriff, don't opt for a skinny jean, go for a mid-to-high waist. If you want to look slimmer, then go for dark wash jeans. Try on as many different styles and brands as time will allow. Given the variety of denims on the market, no one should have to settle for jeans they're not comfortable in.

- Denim really is a specialised subject which is why you're always better off going to a shop that specialises in a large variety of jeans. The staff are usually highly trained and will be able to tell you the kind of jean styles and cuts that will suit your figure.

1. Alexa Chung
2. Christy Turlington

ERIN O'CONNOR, SUPERMODEL

Imagine having Karl Lagerfeld describe you as one of the best models in the world? Or how about Jean Paul Gaultier likening you to art?

Erin O'Connor is one woman who knows exactly what this is like, and yet she remains one of the most unassuming and refreshingly modest people in the industry.

As well as endorsing fair trade fashion, Erin is the vice chair of the British Fashion Council as well as the founder of the phenomenally successful Model Sanctuary, which offers respite and a full-time nutritionist to young models in the business.

An inspiration to women everywhere, Erin has gone from being in the firing line of teenage ridicule to being one of the most influential models worldwide. By her own admission, it was her first-hand experience of people trying to impose their limitations on her that led to her acquiring a genuine sense of self-confidence and aplomb, qualities that set her apart from her contemporaries. What's more, she is completely oblivious to her astounding beauty, which, as many of her fans will agree, makes her even more beautiful.

Recently, I caught up with Erin to discuss everything from her love of vintage to practising couture poses in port-a-loos!

Q. In your early modelling days, you were famously asked to get a boob job and a nose job. What was your reaction to this request at the time? How did you deal with someone judging you like that?

A. Part of a model's job is to be judged and critiqued on a daily basis, so I wasn't entirely surprised. What I didn't like was the idea of someone imposing their own limitations upon me. As a woman, I'm not immune to a bad day

now and then, so when someone tries to tell me what's wrong with me, I'm just not having any of it! When I attended school as a kid, I suffered criticism and was so aware of how acutely different I looked. On the one hand, I was growing spectacularly tall, yet other arrivals were somewhat amiss, i.e. the boob department! I'm not saying I wasn't a little self-conscious about it but, looking back, I really think the boob job suggestion was an invaluable wake-up call. I just thought, well I'm my own version of a woman and I don't need someone telling me what's wrong with my body. In a way, it was a very good experience for me, because it helped me accept exactly who I was.

Q. You appear to have a love of tailored garments. What are your favourite tailored pieces?

A. I'm actually quite a fan of men's vintage tailoring, but I do harbour a love for the tailoring of designers such as Jean Paul Gaultier and Moschino. I love wearing suits because they give me that wonderful feeling of empowerment. I also love how they make me feel so feminine. I actually feel quite delicate within the structure of a suit.

Q. How does it feel to have someone as incredible as Karl Lagerfeld say the most extraordinary things about you? He described you as one of the best and most beautiful models working today!

A. It's definitely a jaw-dropping compliment because one of the things Karl Lagerfeld understands is the relationship between a model and a designer. It's a collaboration. The two of us chatted one day about how passé the notion of 'a muse' has become; it sounds like such a passive role. The reality is that you can't have one without the other – the designer has the imagination, but the model has to bring the garment to life. It was always so much fun working with Karl because he's so funny and rather naughty at times! You often don't incorporate humour with fashion but he was always very good at doing that! He always knew that modelling should be characterful. I've gained a lot of respect for that because I've realised it's most definitely a skill, but one you can develop.

Q. It must be amazing to have garnered the admiration of such amazing people. I read that Jean Paul Gaultier also said of you, "She isn't just a model, she is quite like art, she's like theatre, she's an extraordinary inspiration. I would love to be with her every day."

A. There's something in me that's a bit of a show-off. When I take the stage, it's mine! I'm very unapologetic about that, and the reason for this is because it's not really me that's up there on the runway! I have to very deliberately detach between the real me and the model. When I'm modelling, I'm playing a character. I get a lot of saucy dark characters to play and I have to say they're much easier to play than a goody-

two shoes. I don't know what that says about me though! To do the clothes justice, you have to get into performance mode. Backstage at a fashion show is absolute pandemonium and we often don't even have a mirror to check ourselves in before we walk out on stage. For years, I practised couture poses in port-a-loos! But the reason Jean Paul said I was quite like art is because I'm always playing dead people! Part of a great designer's job is to reference what has already happened historically. Most designers draw inspiration from things like paintings or stories and for me, as a model, I have to try and do justice to these great icons that once lived. It's a huge responsibility but one that I relish. There's a relationship of trust between Jean Paul and me. He creates the most extraordinary things and I love him for it.

Q. I think the next step for you is acting!

A. I beg to differ. I think there's only room for one narcissistic career in a lifetime!

Q. You wrote in your blog on Vogue.com that you were more than happy to celebrate turning thirty. So many women dread this milestone, did you at any point dread the big three zero or was it something that never fazed you? What advice would you have for women approaching a milestone?

A. I have been playing very grown-up, strong women since I was in my late teens, so to have finally arrived at that place in my real life was an absolute victory. I relished it! It felt like my wedding day! I had the mother of all celebrations and I just felt so proud about reaching this milestone. It felt like a place of arrival. The theme of the celebration was love because that's what I was feeling at the time. I felt loved up! I was so unapologetic about the festive celebrations I threw for it. I had a big, themed party and Vivienne Westwood designed my party dress. It was such a lovely experience because all my family and friends arrived from all over the world for it. I think it's really important that as you grow, whether it be growing up or growing old, that you just embrace and remember the key events of your life. Whether they are relevant or not at the time, you will someday look back on them and remember them.

Q. You have often spoken out about embracing your natural porcelain skin and your body shape. In doing so, you have inspired many others, including myself, to follow suit. What do you make of women and young girls who over-tan, be it on the sunbed or with the tanning products?

A. The pressure they feel they're under does upset me. Of course, if women want to apply fake tan or fake nails because it gives them an element of happiness, then each to their own, who am I to stand in their way? But I just want them to think about why they are doing it and what it means to them. Let's just be real here for a moment. Economically speaking, enhancements such as hair and nail extensions, and tanning are going to cost a lot of money long term.

Confidence comes from self-acceptance. Sadly, a lot of women don't think they are beautiful without make-up. I think we sometimes hide behind make-up because, otherwise, we feel very exposed without it. Both men and women seemed to have lost the right to be themselves. We're being told, in an almost dictatorial way, about what's in and what's out and how we should look. It's disturbing and unfair.

Q. You once stated that when you were fifteen years of age, you loved the excitement of looking for "one-off pieces, a second-hand garment with a narrative that nobody else would own". Has that love still remained with you fifteen years on? From what age did you develop such an individual style?

A. I've been spoiled though; look at the industry I work in! When it comes to style, it's not about what's right or wrong, it's about what suits you individually. To coin an old phrase, you can't buy style, it's something that evolves when you become comfortable in your skin.

For example, the irony with me is that I can't do trends, which you would think would be a stumbling block given the career I've entered into. Generally though, I cannot wear trends and I've come to realise that in order to feel fashionable and comfortable, you have to sometimes deny yourself things like platforms and A-Line mini dresses if they don't do you justice.

It also becomes increasingly difficult for women to know how to dress as they get older. Again, we feel trapped because we read magazines and see these must-have items that we feel we should be wearing. My advice is to have a number of staple items in your wardrobe and to adopt trends in the form of accessories. Rather than wearing the leopard print dress, why not instead opt for a pair of leopard print shoes? There are always ways and means. We should all take pride in our fashion disasters and look at them fondly and with affection. You know what? You don't have to be a kid to make those mistakes! Fashion is all about evolving! Let go a little bit and have fun!

Q. What advice would you offer to women with low self-esteem?

A. Stop berating each other. Stop blaming men for not making you feel good about yourselves. The problem is we're still stuck on the idea that we need to present the right attitude rather than giving it. As women, we need to stick together and realise that the one thing we have in common is our differences and that's what makes us unique. Surround yourself with positive people.

Q. Sometimes, our clothes have such interesting stories or some form of sentimental attachment behind them. Is there any item of clothing in your wardrobe that has an interesting story behind it?

A. I'm a recycler and I rarely buy a new piece of clothing – I'm vintage all the way. London is great for vintage and I've also picked up some great items in Dublin and Texas. One of the outfits that will always stand out for me is a dress I treated myself to for my twenty-first birthday. It was Versace couture, long and sparkly and just terribly grown up for a twenty-one year old. I suddenly decided that I wanted to youth it up a little, so I slashed it to the knee and cut the back out!

Q. When you walk the catwalk, you look so confident and self-assured. Would you agree that the right posture and confidence can change a woman's appearance and improve her overall look?

A. I couldn't agree more. Great posture means presence. I think when you walk into a room with good posture and presence, you're not apologising for it and as a result you have more chance of succeeding in the world. If I didn't control the clothes on the catwalk, they would control me. The clothes aren't always terribly manoeuvrable so you have to command them, and I'm a great believer in being quite authoritative on the catwalk because I don't want to look like I'm whimpering within them. I just want to look like an adult in control of myself. I try to hold my own.

Q. So many women, young women in particular, adopt a pout when posing for photographs, however you are often pictured with a broad smile and you have often stated that your successful career in modelling is not just as a result of your looks but your ability to project character and personality. As such, would you encourage young women to ditch the pout and smile more often?

A. Once you stop trying, you become — and feel — more attractive. I know looks are important in the career I'm in, but I haven't got by on my looks at all. I arrived at the tail end of an era where many of the models were worshipped for their beautiful appearance. When we arrived, however, we were like the naughty schoolkids or the extras from *Grange Hill*, but we embodied something totally different. We had a wonderful energy. We weren't asked to pout, pose and linger. It was more about developing personality. I just think we all look so much more attractive when we're relaxed and smiling.

Q. You took a risk by giving up your A-level studies and heading to London to take up modelling. So many women would love to have the courage to pursue an ambition. What words of advice would you give them?

A. I felt immense pressure to follow the correct channels in life such as the A-level route. However, I discussed it with my tutors and my parents and we just decided that modelling would provide me with extraordinary opportunities. It would open a whole new world for me to explore. I also knew the option was there for me to return to school at a later stage, so I took a year out and went for it. Fate intervened and I can't ignore that, because it gave me a wonderful life. Hopefully, it has changed my life, and my family's life, for the better. I'm a great believer in education but different people have different methods of learning and appreciating things. This December, I will be fifteen years in the modelling business and even after all this time, self-education is still an ongoing process.

Slimming Down your Look

"Style is an expression of individualism mixed with charisma. Fashion is something that comes after style."

John Fairchild

There are so many wonderful tips to embrace when it comes to slimming down your look. While no single item of clothing will take away the extra weight, there are various tips you can use to your advantage. When you have armed yourself with the proper knowledge relating to your shape, there is no reason why you can't create the illusion of a slender figure.

1. Beyoncé Knowles
2. Ivanka Trump
3. The shoulder pad look
4. Jennifer Lopez

41

- Go for clothes that drape your body. These are the kind of fabrics that slide close to the skin but don't cling to it. If you wear clothes that cling, you risk showing every lump and bump, whereas if you wear clothing that drapes the skin, you will show off your frame beautifully.

- If you want to downplay a double chin, wear a V-neck top. A good rule of thumb for those looking to disguise a double chin is to keep colour away from the chin area. For instance, turtleneck tops are not a good idea as they can draw attention to the chin as well as making your face look wider.

- If your midriff area is the problem, then wear dark clothing that softly drapes your frame. Dark colours are slimming, but try to brighten your look with a colourful handbag, jewellery or a long skinny scarf.

- Keep your overall look simple. Avoid large pockets, buttons or anything that makes the clothing look bulky.

- If you are of tall stature, a long skirt will not only elongate your frame, it will also make you appear leaner. If you are short in height, however, a long skirt will make you appear even shorter and can sometimes make a person look heavier than what they actually are. A skirt with a knee-high hemline, on the other hand, will make you appear slightly taller and leaner.

- Often, a statement necklace will draw the eye away from your frame, however, jewellery pieces that are either quite bulky or small can sometimes achieve the opposite effect desired. For example, if a larger women wears a small piece of jewellery, it can actually create the illusion that she is heavier than she really is. This is why it's essential that you choose jewellery appropriate to your size. If you are still unsure avoid jewellery that is either quite bulky or particularly small.

- In the same way pointy-toed heels can make you appear taller, they can also make your frame appear leaner, especially if they are a neutral colour. Also, avoid heels with ankle straps as they will cut off the illusion and make your legs appear shorter.

- Regardless of what size you are, good posture and proper breathing are the best ways to achieve an instant lean appearance so stand tall, keep your shoulders back and hold your head up high.

- Straight-legged trousers can really create a leaner look. When investing in a good pair of trousers, go for a pair with a waistline that sits just below your navel. If the waistline starts to gather, then it is too tight. If the waist line is too low, it will give you the dreaded muffin top look. The only way to correctly judge trousers is to try them out by

Helen Mirren wearing jewellery to complement her style.

sitting down, standing up and walking the shop floor. Make sure you can move comfortably and that everything stays in place.

- Feminine A-line dresses (these are narrow at the top and slightly flare out towards the bottom thereby resembling the letter A) are fantastic for disguising problem areas and flattering the figure.

- "Dressing from head to toe in the one colour is the best way to create the illusion of a slim figure." While this may be somewhat true, it does not mean that you have to limit your wardrobe to dark colours. Wrap dresses, for instance, look beautiful whether they are in purple, red, black or blue.

- Although vertical and horizontal stripes should be avoided as they can sometimes create the illusion that a person is slightly heavier than they are, patterns such as diagonal stripes and zigzags can actually distract the eye away from problem areas.

- Fashion designers and stylists always look at the body as a blank canvas. Remember, if the canvas is smooth, the finished result will be equally as smooth in appearance. This means investing in the appropriate underwear and wearing it correctly. Bra straps that are too tight will cause back rolls not to mention bulging underarm skin.

- Meanwhile briefs that are ill fitting will cause the dreaded VPL. While they may not look particularly appealing, the proper undergarments can help slim your overall appearance as well as enhance your confidence. Body slimmers and shapers are fantastic for pulling in any excess weight and making you feel slender. Often women don't realise that there is a wide variety of undergarments out there to cater for every problematic area whether it be the midriff, arms or legs.

- Spanx Underwear is a brand well known for its slimming results and while it was always associated with under garments, the good news is that it has now extended its range to swimwear as well. If you enjoy swimming and being involved in water sports but feel self-conscious in a bathing suit, my advice would be to shop around and seek out the many different varieties available for every individual requirement. If you feel uncomfortable with your thighs for instance, then look out for stylish swim shorts that are actually veiled underneath a small beach skirt thereby giving you the freedom to swim and walk the beach in confidence.

Tips to suit your shape

Regardless of whether you are a size twelve or a size twenty, if the fit is wrong, your clothes will not hang correctly. If you wear an item that's too baggy, you will look larger, whereas if you wear something that is too tight or small, it will cling to your frame and highlight any problematic areas. The key is to find the right fit.

Top heavy

Top-heavy women are often very conscious of their upper halves but heeding the right tricks can make the world of difference to both your appearance and your confidence.

- If you are heavier on the upper part of your body, then choose tops that are of loose fitting which slim down to cinch the hips and waist.

- Opt for thin fabrics, such as cotton or cotton jersey, which won't add bulk.

- Choose long jackets that do not have shoulder pads.

- Create the illusion of length by sticking to one colour.

- Try a knee length pleated or patterned skirt to bring the eye down to your lower half.

Ivanka Trump

Bottom heavy

The key to dressing a bottom-heavy figure is balance. When you get this right, you will never again struggle with style.

- If you are carrying weight on the lower part of your body, one of the best ways to even out your frame is to wear a top or jacket with small shoulder pads.

- Dark trousers or jeans are also quite good for minimising the lower part of your frame.

- Limit prints to the upper part of your body only.

- Look for jackets, dresses and tailored suits with straight, classic cuts.

- Long, fitted tops that go past your hips are always a great option.

Hourglass

If you are blessed with an hourglass figure, the best thing you can do is emphasise it by wearing styles and fabrics that show off your body.

- Highlight your waist with a large belt, a corset or a waist nipper.

- If you are not particularly comfortable with your curves, try wearing a fitted V-neck top. This will give structure to your shape while at the same time drawing the eye upwards towards the face.

- Asymmetric (or one-shouldered) tops or dresses are beautiful if you want to draw attention to a different part of your body while, at the same time, maintaining your overall shape. Kate Winslet has pioneered this look in recent times.

- Before you buy an item, walk around in it and ensure that it moves with you and your curves. Always wear the clothes, don't let them wear you.

Not-so-curvy

If you're not particularly curvy, there are a number of ways in which you can add some dimension to your frame.

- Wearing patterns is a great option.

- Draw attention to your face, and away from your body, by wearing statement pieces such as dramatic jackets or colourful earrings or scarves.

- Slightly loose-patterned clothing, such as a floral dress, can be quite good for drawing the eye away from your body shape.

- To enhance your upper half, blouses with adornments such as ruffles and embellishments will create a fuller illusion. Layering may look like an art form, but when you get it right, the result it worth it.

- Jeans with bulky pockets are often a good solution when it comes to creating the illusion of a fuller lower half. Puffball skirts are also a brilliant choice when it comes to achieving that 'fuller' look.

- Look out for different varieties of body shaping under garments that can help add contour to your body.

Items to avoid

If you are uncomfortable with your weight, there are particular items of clothing that should be avoided regardless of what shape you are.

- Tight clingy dresses can often accentuate the wrong areas of the body.

- Flowing tops can sometimes give the illusion of a baby bump when there isn't one. This is often the case with empire waistlines.

- Baggy clothes.

- Large patterns, especially stripes.

- Low-rise pants bring with them a high risk of the dreaded muffin top look.

Styling those Curves

Back when I was a bigger size, I developed a habit of dressing around my weight so that no one would see my true size. I just found it so difficult to source nice clothes that would flatter my shape and improve my confidence. At the time, it seemed like there was nothing stylish for women with curves which was incredibly disheartening. Fortunately, however, fashion has come a long way since then and things have changed for the better. These days, there is an array of beautiful clothes on the market that are tailored to suit curvy women. Of course, the trick is knowing how to work the items to suit your individual shape.

CURVY FRAME

- If you are lucky enough to have well-proportioned curves all over, then start emphasising them! Do you ever see Beyoncé hiding her curves underneath baggy tops and shirts? Never! Everything she wears is fitted to support and flatter her shape. Follow Beyoncé's lead and start dressing to enhance your curves rather than hide them.

- Fitted V-neck's are very comfortable and are ideal for smoothing over curves.

- Pencil skirts were made for curvaceous ladies! Pair the skirt with a fitted V-neck or shirt and you have a stylish look that will take you anywhere. The added advantage of pencil skirts is that they cinch the waist and make you appear slimmer and taller.

- Wrap dresses are extremely elegant and are wonderful for skimming the curves without clinging to them.

- Accessorising with a belt is a great way of accentuating the waist if you are tall and curvy. Unfortunately, if you are under five feet in height, wearing a belt will cut your figure in half, making you appear shorter.

- A-line dresses and skirts flatter most figures and are particularly good for disguising bottom-heavy figures. They are extremely elegant and will enhance your curves beautifully.

Beyoncé Knowles

CURVY MIDRIFF

"I want to be a voluptuous woman with curves."

Cameron Diaz

- If like most women, you are conscious of your midriff, chances are you find it difficult to source nice-fitting tops. The trick, however, is in the sleeve! Look for loose-fitting tops with slim-fitting sleeves. The flowing section of the top will give you breathing room while the sleeves will give you a nice, slim shape.

- If you want a skirt that disguises your midriff, then look for skirts that are slightly pleated. The pleats draw the attention away from the stomach area of your body. Likewise, asymmetric necklines will also detract from the midriff area.

- Those who are conscious of their stomach area should steer clear of empire waistlines as these can sometimes add weight and give you the 'pregnant look'. A-line dresses are a much better option.

CURVY THIGHS

"In life, as in art, the beautiful moves in curves."

Robert Bulwer Lytton

- If you want to wear dresses and skirts but are conscious of your thighs, try wearing opaque tights. These are wonderful for slimming the leg and are a fantastic solution for anyone who dislikes their lower half.

- Look for long tops that reach as far as the top of your thigh. Tops that are slightly flared at the bottom are even better for disguising troublesome thighs.

- Stay away from pencil skirts as these will only emphasise the thigh area. A-line dresses and skirts are so much more elegant and are perfect for bottom-heavy figures.

Jennifer Lopez

Tips for Petite Women

For some petite ladies, sourcing style can prove a difficult task. To some degree, the term 'petite' is misunderstood. Contrary to popular belief, not all women of petite stature wear XS, as petite is all about height and not weight. In fact, only those who are five foot four inches and under are considered petite. The good news, however, is that there are many tricks petite women can avail of when it comes to creating the illusion of height.

AVOID OVERSIZED ACCESSORIES

Avoid those large handbags and sunglasses you often see being sported by celebrities. Oversized items such as these can overwhelm a petite woman and leave her looking shorter than she really is. Instead, opt for medium-sized handbags so that they don't look out of proportion to your height. When it comes to sunglasses, speak to an optician about finding the right sized frames for your face.

NARROW BELTS

If you are wearing a belt, ensure it is of the slim kind and, if possible, the same colour as your top. Wide or contrasting belts cut the figure in half and break up the vertical illusion that you need to achieve in order to appear taller.

SOLID COLOURS

Wearing just one colour from head to toe is a well-known way to create the illusion of height.

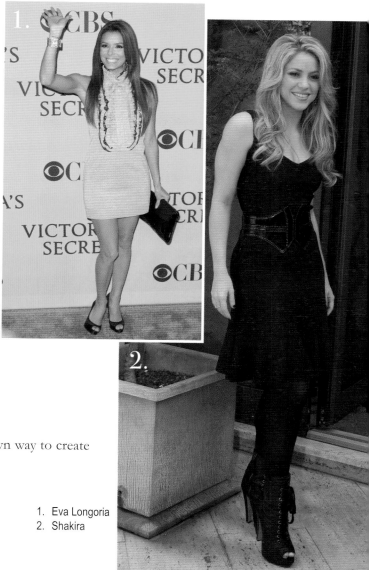

1. Eva Longoria
2. Shakira

TROUSERS WITH STRAIGHT LEGS

Wear jeans and trousers with straight legs and stay away from bell bottoms and wide-legged pants. Instead, look for trousers that are tailored, such as straight leg or slim bootcut styles.

The waistband of your trousers should sit comfortably across the top of your hips; never below them or you risk making your hips look wider than they actually are. Avoid at all costs high-waist trousers as they will cover up most of your torso, thereby making you appear shorter.

KNEE-HIGH HEMLINES

If you are shopping for skirts or dresses, make sure the hemline hits just above the knee or on the knee itself. Calf-length skirts are extremely unflattering on petite women and do nothing to elongate the frame. A-line or pencil skirts are always flattering.

VERTICAL PRINTS

Avoid garments with horizontal lines. These will only add width to your shape and make you look shorter than you are.

Instead, look for clothes that have strong vertical lines. These include zip-front styles, ribbed knits and wrap styles. In fact, anything with zippers will create a strong vertical line on your petite frame which is exactly what you want. Remember vertical lines are a great way of creating the illusion of length.

PRINT SIZES

Large prints can often overpower a small frame which is why it's always a better idea to opt for small prints. If you are unsure about whether a print is the right size for you, then bear in mind the following rule: if the pattern is larger than your fist, then the print is too big for your frame. When it comes to animal prints, keep it to a minimum.

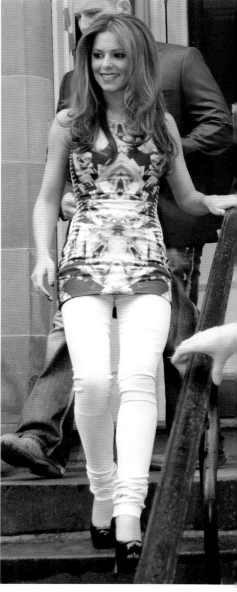

Petite Cheryl Cole keeps her prints small and her trouser legs straight.

V-Necklines

A V-neckline always makes a short body frame look longer (on that note a hip-length top is also fantastic for lengthening the torso too).

Bright colours

Bright colours worn above the waist will create a high focal point thus adding to the illusion of height. Likewise, details such as embroidery, sequins, beading, lace or faux fur featured on your top half will also draw attention upwards for added height. An embellished neckline, for example, will immediately draw the eye upwards.

Empire waistlines

A slim-fitting dress or top with an empire waist is a petite woman's best friend. 'Empire waist' is the term used when the waistline on the garment is raised above the natural waistline of the body, sometimes as high as right below the bust. It works best on women who are quite slim on top or who have petite frames as it adds to the illusion of height. For some women, the empire waist can leave them with the 'pregnant' look. If this is the case for you, then try cinching the empire waist with a skinny belt.

Eva Longoria

Be careful with maxi dresses

Women with petite frames have long been led to believe they cannot pull off the maxi dress trend. Fortunately, thanks to the wide range of styles on offer, this is not the case anymore. The trick is knowing which maxis to avoid.

- Stay away from maxis that smother your figure and leave you looking shorter than you are. Instead, look for a maxi dress that is full length and sits close to your body. Petite women need structured dresses so it's always a good idea to wear a maxi dress with an empire waist.

- A maxi dress with a V-neckline will elongate a short frame in the same way as a V-neck top.

- Look for maxi dresses in solid colours, such as black, purple, brown red or yellow.

- Above all, avoid horizontal and large patterns.

The right shoes

When a petite woman looks to elongate her frame, her first port of call is usually the high-heeled stock of the shoe shops. Sometimes, however, a high heel isn't enough to complete the illusion of height.

- Try to look for shoes that are either pointed or open-toed, however stay away from ankle straps as they visually cut off the length of your lower legs.

- Avoid wearing flat shoes with skirts that hit below the knee. Needless to say, wearing stilettos every day is not realistic which is why it's always a good idea to instead invest in wedges with cushioned soles.

- Stay clear of thigh-high boots, as these will only make you look shorter than you are. Thigh high boots are best suited to taller women.

- Strapless nude shoes are wonderful for creating the illusion of a longer leg.

Salma Hayek uses her strapless nude shoes to create the illusion of a longer frame.

The right jeans

When it comes to jeans, Levi, Lee and Gloria Vanderbilt are a few of the brands which offer a petite cut.

Add structure

It's best to keep away from large shapeless tops as these will smother your frame. Instead, opt for tailored tops that possess a structure aimed at flattering your figure. To elongate your upper body visually, choose open necklines, such as V-necks or scoop necks.

Be selective with accessories

Petite woman should always avoid chokers and cuff bracelets. Long necklaces on the other hand are to be embraced. Accessories such as a broach can be used to draw the eye upwards thus creating the perception of height. Long skinny scarves are also ideal for the petite woman as they create vertical lines on the figure and keep the focal point high. On this note, petite women should steer clear of short bulky scarves.

Walk tall

Even if you incorporate all the tips above, you will immediately undo all your good work if you walk around with your shoulders slumped. If you want to look taller, the most important thing is good posture.

Ashley Olsen works the height trick with a long scarf.

Petite celebrities

Many Hollywood A-listers are members of the petite club, yet you will never see them being held back by their height when it comes to style. In fact, most of them are style icons and regularly make it on to the 'best dressed' lists.

Despite being only five-feet one-inch tall, actress Eva Longoria Parker exemplifies impeccable style regardless of whether she is attending an awards ceremony or in the character of Gabrielle Solis on the set of *Desperate Housewives*. Meanwhile, standing at just five feet, it's no wonder Australian singer Kylie Minogue is often referred to as 'pint sized', yet this has never stopped her possessing a sense of style envied by most women.

Likewise Renée Zellweger, at five feet four inches, has been a firm fixture on Vanity Fair's International Best Dressed List. It just goes to prove that style is not limited to those of supermodel stature.

1. Nicole Ritchie
   5 feet 1 inch
2. Jodie Foster
   5 feet 3 inches
3. Reese Witherspoon
   5 feet 2 inches
4. Helen Mirren
   5 feet 4 inches

Dressing a Tall Frame

While we all may envy the height of supermodels, we often fail to realise that even our runway favourites have, more than likely, cursed their stature at some point in their lives.

"I used to wear heels because I wanted to show people I wasn't ashamed of being tall."

Elle MacPherson

Gisele Bundchen, Tyra Banks, Elle MacPherson and even the supremely confident actress Sigourney Weaver have all been self-conscious about their height at some stage. However, like so many other women, they too have come to realise the many advantages of being tall. As a result, they are now happier and more confident with their bodies.

If you are self-conscious about your height, the many tips outlined below can help you visually shorten your frame. To be honest, though, I would advise that you try and make the most of what you have. Your height is permanent so why not appreciate it instead of trying to hide it? Look upon your stature not as a flaw but as an asset.

The first thing tall women need to realise is that most people generally don't pay much attention to the height of others. If you're particularly self-conscious, chances are you are convincing yourself that everyone is staring at you when, in fact, they probably haven't even noticed your height. Embrace your stature and actively begin training yourself to stop worrying about standing out.

Always remember, the only accessories needed to finish any outfit beautifully are good posture and confidence.

WEAR MAXI DRESSES

These are wonderful for tall women. Whether you choose to pair the dress with ballet flats, wedges or gladiator sandals, it's a look that works beautifully on women with added height. If, however, you feel that a long dress will elongate your frame even more, then wear a belt across your midriff. This will instantly break the look in half, making you appear less tall as a result.

USE YOUR HAIR

Wear your hair down as up-styles can add to the illusion of a longer frame.

Your lengths

A longer top will almost always shorten your legs visually. Tunic tops and T-shirts that are hip length are vital must-haves. In summer, Capri pants are a brilliant addition to your wardrobe as they look fantastic on tall women. Also, if you are very conscious of being tall, then steer clear of tight fitting clothes as they will only accentuate your height even further.

Mix your colours

Mixing light and dark shades will break the illusion of length. For example, wear a dark top with light blue jeans just like Miss five-feet-eleven Sophie Dahl.

Avoid pinstripes

These add to the illusion of length and will make you appear taller. Instead choose horizontal stripes over vertical. Be careful with horizontal stripes if you are conscious of your weight as they could make you appear somewhat heavier.

Open necklines

When buying tops, avoid necklines that are too close to your neck, including turtlenecks. Wearing these will only elongate your torso in an unflattering way. Instead, opt for ruffles, V-necks, shirts or scoop necks to visually break the length of the torso.

Fitted jeans

Invest in a good pair of fitted jeans. Jeans that are tailored to your height will do wonders for your frame. Skinny jeans are particularly flattering on women with long, thin legs.

Rachel Hunter

SHOW OFF YOUR LEGS

If you are blessed with long legs show them off but just make sure you cover up your bust. The golden rule is 'one or the other'. Remember, though, height doesn't necessarily mean long legs. Some women are six feet tall but still have relatively short legs as their length is mostly in the torso area.

WEAR HEELS

Even if you're six feet tall, high heels are still an option. In fact, women like Sophie Dahl, Rebecca Romijn, and Rachel Hunter are living proof that tall women can enjoy high heels. It depends on how comfortable you are with your height. If you do go for those stilettos, remember to be extra careful, walking in high heels tends to be more difficult for tall women.

SHOP ONLINE

More and more shops are catering for tall women however, the best selection of clothes remain online. Whether you are searching for a pair of jeans or a wedding dress, it's worth browsing the web for a range of stylish offers.

WATCH YOUR POSTURE

Tall women have a habit of slouching either because they are trying to downplay their height or because they are always speaking to people shorter than themselves. Sometimes, people slouch out of habit, but if you make a good effort you can adopt a new posture that won't leave you at risk of future back problems. On that note, the next time you plan a holiday, look up www.seatguru.com. This site will give you information on airlines that have seats with extra leg room for tall passengers.

Tall celebrities

1. Elle MacPherson
   6 feet
2. Rebecca Romijn
   5 feet 11 inches
3. Alessandra Ambrosio
   5 feet 10 inches
4. Sigourney Weaver
   5 feet 11 inches

Enhancing Your Style

The Science of Shopping

I think a lot of women go shopping for clothes with the wrong attitude. They treat it like they would a lazy day – then they walk into a shop and expect to find something that looks good on them. Whether it's high-end designer or high street, there isn't anything that could possibly look good on them because they haven't approached their shopping trip with the right mentality.

I'm not suggesting you dress up like you would for a night out, but it would be a good idea to slick on a little bit of bronzer, some lip gloss and to keep your hairstyle neat. Wedges are fantastic to wear when shopping as they still give you the added height but without the pain!

In this section, I am going to share with you all the tips I have learned. From how to navigate the shop floor and work the dressing room to sourcing inspiration for new styles and saving money, it's all in this section.

"Women usually love what they buy, yet they hate two thirds of what's in their wardrobe."

Mignon McLaughlin

HEY, BIG SPENDER – STOP SPENDING FOOLISHLY!

"Shopping with a credit card is much like being drunk. The buzz happens immediately and gives you a lift … The hangover comes the day after."

Joyce Brothers

I don't spend money trying out products, I ask for samples. It might sound like I'm penny pinching but I would much rather use up my samples instead of wasting money on products that may not achieve any results.

I will only buy the product if the sample convinces me it suits my skin.

It's the same with perfume. I always try out the samples first because the scent on the tester sheet can sometimes smell totally different after it has been applied to my skin. Perfume reacts differently to each individual, which is why it's always a good idea to spritz the tester on your wrist and let it sit for a while. See how you take to it and then decide if you still like it enough to buy it.

Everyone can save money in one way or another. I take great care of my shoes. I polish them, I have them mended and heeled and, as a result, they last me four or five seasons. Every birthday and Christmas, my family always know that my present of choice is a shopping voucher. I then combine the vouchers together and buy a good-quality handbag. Classics never date and, as a result, I have built up a collection over the years.

Some people stay away from boutiques because they assume the stock is all designer, but sometimes boutiques are the best places for a bargain. It never fails to amaze me just how many women are intimidated by boutiques. I have met plenty of women who just can't seem to summon up the courage to take that step inside the front door. This is a form of fear – but one that can be overcome. Ladies, it doesn't matter how much money you have or don't have; there is no reason why you can't walk in and try on all the items that catch your eye. Stand strong in your own skin and have the confidence to walk in with your head held high. Do it once and the fear will fade; do it twice and the fear will begin to disappear completely. Before you know it you will be rocking in and out of those boutiques with attitude and confidence. Treat it as a challenge, as a way of improving your self-esteem. Face down your fear and go for it.

Window inspiration

Shop windows are an amazing source of inspiration.

I always find it's worth taking the time to examine the outfits in the window and to see how the different colours and items were put together and accessorised.

Sometimes, a shop will adopt a simplistic look for their window while, on other occasions, it may display a very dramatic couture theme. Either way, staff tend to put their heart and soul into promoting their products in the window, so it's in your interest to scrutinise the outfit in its entirety and, above all, to be inspired by what you see.

Another form of inspiration is the location of the items on the shop floor. Often, clothes and colours that work well together will be displayed beside each other in the shop. This is entirely for your benefit. When you see a shirt on a shop rail and trousers on the rail beside it, this is usually because the two looks have been manufactured to work together. The downside to this is that you might see twenty other people in the street with the same look. If I were buying the shirt, my preference would be to find my own look to go with it – however, that's not to say I wouldn't take the time to see what items the shop had selected to go with it. Always be open to new creative ideas.

Hanger appeal

When people are shopping, they need to realise that some clothes will have absolutely no hanger appeal but will look amazing when they are worn – and even more when they are accessorised. This is why it's so important to really look at everything on the rails. Don't skim over items just because they're not normally the style you would go for. Examine them and envisage yourself wearing them.

So many people think they know what they like and run to what they know. This is how they become stuck in a look – they are not opening themselves up to new styles. Fashion may be my job, but even I can't walk into a shop and know instantly which items I am going to like. I have to root through the rails and have a good look.

You don't have to spend a fortune to look good. For instance, Burberry is known for the elegant trench-coat look, but you can easily recreate the Burberry look with a simple beige mac from the high street. It's all about keeping your eyes open and being inspired. There are fantastic colours out there in terms of shoes, bags and fabrics.

On that note, I can't emphasise enough just how important it is to look and feel the fabrics. Aim for quality all the way. Sometimes, people see the price tag and immediately conclude that it's out of their price range. What they need to realise, however, is that the one thing that costs a little bit more is the very item they will probably wear for years. Weigh up all the pros and cons, but allow the deciding question to be this: does the quality and potential longevity of the item merit the price being asked?

Shopping habits

For some reason, when people walk into a shop, they tend to automatically walk to the right-hand side of the shop and begin their browsing there. If the background music is quite fast, they will whiz around the shop, however if the music is too slow, they will become quite lazy and won't bother trying anything on. Ideally, there should be a balance however if there isn't, you need to pause and remind yourself what you are shopping for. Never be afraid to use the sales assistants for advice and tips. They are there to help you, look after you and service you – so don't ever feel intimidated.

Navigating the shop floor

Don't you hate it when you spend twenty minutes in the dressing room only to suddenly spot something you like as you leave the shop? You almost always end up saying to yourself, 'No, it's too late, I won't bother.'

Surprisingly, a lot of people make this mistake but, with the right browsing plan, it's one that can be avoided. Start by looking at the clothes on the rails along the walls before looking through the rails in the centre of the shop. When you have finished, you will be content knowing that you have seen everything the shop has to offer. It pays to prepare.

One of the signs that you've really made it in the modelling industry is when people immediately know you by your first name. Gisele, Cindy, Elle, Naomi and, of course, Caprice.

Born in California as Caprice Valerie Bourret, the world was first introduced to the beauty when she became a Wonderbra model at the age of twenty-five. Even though Caprice is still very much in demand as a model, the realist inside her understood years ago that the lifespan of a modelling career was short and fleeting. As a result, Caprice turned her name into a brand and from that point onwards, she was seen as a business woman first and a model second.

Personally, I have always admired both her determination to think of big ideas and her unceasing will to make each and every one of them succeed. Testament to her success in the business world are the many invitations she receives to speak about her emergence as an entrepreneur and the pressures of the economy on businesses. Two of her most notable speaking engagements took place in Cambridge University and the London School of Economics.

Caprice took some time from her insanely busy schedule to discuss everything from beauty tips to her unfailingly feminine lingerie collection.

Q. What are your top tips when it comes to maintaining beauty?

A. I don't drink any juices, not even orange juice, because they're full of sugar and, as I always say, sugar is death. I drinks tons of water and I try to get as much sleep as possible. I also try to steer clear of caffeine as well.

Hair, skin and nails will always become immune to the same products if you use them too often so, with this in mind, I change my products every two months. I always try to use organic because with all the toxicity and craziness in the world, not to mention the number of products we use on our skin and hair, I just think it's so much better to use completely natural ingredients. For instance, I use Neem oil on my face and when I want a deep conditioner for my hair, I use flaxseed oil. You basically put the flaxseed oil in your hair and wrap it in clingfilm or secure it under a shower cap. Keep it on for the night and the following morning, shampoo and rinse. Your hair will feel so shiny and soft. I have so many tricks like that! You don't have

to spend a lot to look fabulous, you just have to put in the effort.

In my twenties, I didn't have much to worry about. When I turned thirty, however, things went a bit haywire! Your metabolism slows down and you really have to start taking care of yourself. I now have a really good diet, I take fifty-one vitamins a day, I play tennis twice a week, I go to a trainer twice a week and I also have facials. There is no quick fix; you have to do the work because it's not going to happen otherwise. As you get older, it gets harder. This is why it's important to start young. You shouldn't wait until everything starts to go downhill before you start taking care of yourself. Things won't suddenly reverse, it doesn't work like that. You also can't go through life regularly smoking and drinking and not expect it to catch up with you.

Tip from Caprice

"When I want a deep conditioner for my hair, I use flaxseed oil. You put the flaxseed oil in your hair and secure it under a shower cap. Keep it on for the night and the following morning, shampoo and rinse. Honest to God, your hair will feel so shiny and soft."

Q. What should women look for when buying swimwear? Should they look for longevity?

A. In order to give my customers the products they want, I have to really understand them and their demands. Right now, they want a lot for their money. I'm taking a hit on my margins but customers want good design, quality, originality, not to mention a bloody good price, and that's what I'm giving them!

Every woman's body is very different, so variety is also important. This is why I provide such an extensive range – for example, I have swimwear that is low waist, high waist, one-piece swimsuits, two-piece sets, and many more.

When it comes to fashion and trends, women shouldn't let the magazines to dictate what looks good. Instead, they should look at what suits them and makes them feel sexy. As modern women, we want a style that empowers us.

Q. What first inspired you to create swimwear and underwear? Did you see a niche in the market?

A. At the time, I was in my early thirties and I had to be realistic with myself. I knew that modelling was not going to last for ever and I had to think of the future. I considered the various markets that I could break into and then I began to think about the underwear market. Initially, I wanted to do a licence deal with an established company so I called Terry Greene who was head of Debenhams at the time. Nobody was doing licence deals back then so Terry was intrigued and he took my appointment. I'm so persistent I could sell anything and, as a result, Terry went with my idea. I had my licence deal for five years and, afterwards, I bought back my licence and started up my own company.

Q. When do you start designing for the next season? How far in advance does the work start?

A. We work far in advance. For instance, in May 2010, I got the final samples of the 2011 spring/summer collection. I drop a new collection every three months. I also test run all the bras myself. When it comes to a brand, people like to see new items on a regular basis so I am all the time planning new and fresh designs. I used to have a facilitator, a middle-man, but I couldn't afford the margin because of the economy so, now, I'm just doing everything myself. In a way, that's a good thing because it means there's a lot more originality. I find that most designers attend a school of design and, as a result, all of their products look the same, but ever since I began to do things on my own, my sales have been even better. It's a lot of work but of all my accolades, this is the one thing that I'm proudest of because I work my hardest at it.

Q. Take us through a typical day in your life?

A. That's a bit challenging because there really is no one typical day! I could be in Ireland filming for twelve hours one day and then flying over to London for business meetings the next day. Home for me is on a plane! I base myself in London but I do spend a lot of time in the States as well.

Q. Given your extensive experience in the modelling industry, what tips would you offer to women in relation to posing for the camera?

A. Look in the mirror and do your homework. If you want to look your absolute best in photographs, then you have to realise that there's more to posing than just looking into the camera and smiling. Look into the mirror and figure out what angles work for you – stand at a left angle or a right angle, tilt your head, do everything! I don't have the longest legs but I

know how to make them appear long because I've looked in the mirror and played around with the different poses. I even had my assistant take pictures of my different poses so that I could see what looked best in photographs. It's my job as a model to make other people's clothes look fabulous so I practised my poses to make sure I get it absolutely right.

Q. Can you describe your style?

A. My style changes frequently. A lot of women don't change their style as they mature which is a big mistake. In my twenties and early thirties, I had a rock and roll look. Actually, it was gross and, looking back, I think it was also a little bit tacky. Now that I'm thirty-eight years old, I go for a more tailored look. I love suits and classic, elegant, timeless styles.

When it comes to public events, I love dressing up. I'm usually loaned gowns because the designers know I will be photographed in their sample. The gown is always handed back the following day though!

Q. What tips would you offer to women in terms of lingerie?

A. Nine times out of ten, women are not wearing the right size bra. If it's uncomfortable, don't put up with it, get measured and wear the proper size. Even I was wearing the wrong size bra at one point, but when I got measured and began wearing the right size, it made such a huge difference to my appearance.

Realistically, every woman has a black bra and a white bra for different outfits however, it's good to have a nude bra in your collection as well. Of course, it's always nice to have some fashionable pieces to make you feel fabulous.

Lingerie

I say it all the time, if you want to drastically improve your appearance, you have to begin with your underwear. After all, they're not known as foundation garments for nothing!

"If you are wearing lingerie that makes you feel glamorous, you're halfway there to turning heads."

Elle MacPherson

BRAS

A large number of women stick to the one kind of bra regardless of the outfit they are wearing. Considering the variety of underwear on the market, this is completely unnecessary not to mention a huge mistake. If you're wearing the wrong kind of bra – or worse, the wrong size – your clothes will just not sit right.

More often than not, a woman's reliance on the old favourites comes from an unwillingness to embrace the new styles. With so many different lingerie terms, the underwear department may seem quite overwhelming at first. However, when you know the different results produced by the various bras, you should have no problem finding the right ones for you.

For instance, if you want to downplay a big bust, then you need to look for a bust-minimising bra. This will still give your breasts a great shape without further emphasising them. If you have large breasts (E, F, G and upwards) you should always go for full cup bras as they will offer the adequate support for your bust.

If, on the other hand, you have a small bust and want to create the illusion of bigger cleavage, then you need to wear a plunge bra or a balcony bra.

To make your search easier, I have compiled a lingerie dictionary which you will find at the end of this section!

Remember what your mother said...

We are reminded time and time again about the importance of wearing a bra that is the correct size, but yet how many of us have actually paid heed? Very few of us it would seem, as this continues to be one of the most common mistakes made by women.

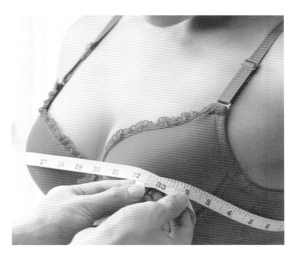

Various factors in our lives, such as our age and weight, can contribute greatly to our bust size. As our bodies change, our bra requirements also change and so a proper fitting is necessary to take these changes into account and to determine whether or not you will need a bra that provides extra support, better fit or wider straps.

At the other end of the spectrum, there are women who wear bras two sizes too small in a bid to achieve a bigger push-up look. This is neither attractive nor necessary, and usually only ever results in the bust spilling over the bra, leaving the woman with underarm and back cleavage.

When it comes down to achieving a certain look with a bra, the trick is knowing which bras offer which results.

Girls, trust me. When you start wearing the right bras for your bust size, you immediately kiss goodbye to all those little niggling problems such as straps constantly falling down, boob spillage and discomfort. Your bra should feel like a second skin, and for me that means the comfort factor is mandatory. You won't achieve this, however, unless you get fitted by a professional who can guide you towards the best bras for your bust and body shape.

How you wear it makes all the difference

When you try on a bra, you have to adjust it in a number of different ways before you can decide if it's really giving you the results you want.

This might sound like common sense but a lot of women do not wear their bras correctly. Firstly, your bra straps should be neither too tight or too loose. You should be able to fit just two fingers underneath the shoulder straps.

Next, fit yourself into the bra. Scoop in the underarm cleavage and adjust the cups so that they are providing your bust with the adequate coverage. At this point, both the front and back of the bra should be parallel. If the back of the bra is very high up, it will need to be readjusted. The sales assistant helping you with your bra fitting should be able to remedy this problem for you.

If, after all that, you still find you have to adjust your bra, then take it as a sign that you are more than likely wearing the wrong size.

Posture is a major factor when it comes to making the most of your bust. For instance, a padded bra is a godsend if you are naturally small chested and want to enjoy the appearance of a bigger cleavage. If, however, you tend to slouch when you walk, then there is absolutely no point in even buying a padded bra. To really enhance your bust line, you need to keep your shoulders back and walk with good posture. Believe me, posture is everything.

DRESSING TO SUIT YOUR BUST SHAPE

If you have a big bust

- Avoid dresses and tops with a halter neck. This particular style will not offer adequate support for your cleavage and it's very unlikely it will sit right on your frame.

- Avoid long necklaces and wide belts if you want to draw attention away from your bust. Empire waistlines are also completely out.

- Wear a strong dark colour on top and a lighter colour for the bottom half.

- Steer clear of tops that have quite a lot of ruffles or pleats. These will only make your bust appear even larger.

- Wrap dresses are incredibly flattering on women with big busts. Solid dark colours will minimise the appearance of your bust however if you prefer more detail, try to go for vertical prints rather than horizontal.

- Avoid wearing bras with too much lace or embellishments, otherwise you run the risk of your bust appearing larger.

- Sleeveless tops can sometimes draw attention towards the bust, however tops with three-quarter length sleeves will usually take the focus away.

- When shopping for a blouse or a shirt, look for one that is fitted at the waist and slightly loose at the bust.

If you have a small bust

- If you want to enhance your cleavage, try a padded balcony bra. A balcony bra is often far more flattering for a small bust than a push-up bra. Corsets are also wonderful for women who want a more defined bust and waist.

- If you are very conscious of your bust size, try diverting attention away from the area. Try wearing a one-shouldered top or, better still, pair a strapless top with a dramatic choker or necklace. A halter-neck top, particularly one with an embellished neckline, is the ideal solution for a woman who wants to direct attention away from her bust line.

- When buying swimwear, shop around. Many brands offer padded swimwear which will give your bust a more defined shape.

- If you are wearing a low-cut top, use bronzer to lightly shade the top of the bust line. This will create the illusion of a fuller cleavage.

- If you don't like the padding in cleavage enhancing bras, try a gel bra or a water bra.

- Tops with medium-sized patterns or horizontal stripes are brilliant for creating the illusion of a bigger bust.

- Avoid tops that are too tight as they will only make your bust appear smaller.

HOSIERY

When you hear the word 'nylon', you immediately think of hosiery items, such as tights and stockings. However, when the creator of nylon came up with the name, he was in fact thinking of New York and London! The 'ny' part of the name refers to initials for New York, while the 'lon' refers to London!

When nylons (as the stockings quickly became known) first emerged in 1940, they hit the fashion world with a bang. In fact over 70,000 pairs of nylon stockings were sold within hours of going on sale in New York. Back then, most stockings were made of silk and had a visible seam running up the back of the leg (when women could not afford these, they would instead draw a vertical line up along the back of their legs in an attempt to recreate the effect).

Top Tip

To reduce the risk of a ladder appearing in your tights, spray a new pair of tights with hairspray. Concentrate on the toes and thighs as these are the two places where the ladders usually begin. The hairspray strengthens the threads in the tights and, as a result, they are stronger and last longer.

Only wear this style if you are blessed with slim legs. If you are carrying weight on your lower half, the visible seam will only emphasise it even more. Likewise tights with a pale or white sheen will add weight to your legs, whereas tights with a slight tan will create the illusion of long, slim legs. To really lengthen your legs, however, wear nude or flesh-coloured hosiery with nude-coloured, strapless shoes.

CARING FOR YOUR UNDERWEAR

Regardless of whether you spend a lot or a little on any given item of underwear, it's how you care for it that will determine its longevity.

- The best way to wash your delicates is by hand, but, of course, this isn't always possible. There's no harm putting them into the washing machine as long as you place them in a washing bag to keep them separate from your other clothes. If you don't have a washing bag, improvise by using a light pillowcase. Just make sure you secure it with a rubber band before placing it in the washing machine.

- When washing briefs, follow the care instruction on the label and use only cool or warm water. Strong heat tends to break down elastic. This is precisely why you should never place bras or briefs in the tumble dryer. Instead, allow them to air dry. This will increase their longevity.

- When washing your shape wear, keep it away from hot water and the tumble dryer as the high temperatures will destroy the controlling performance of the garment.

- When washing underwear, never overload the washing bag, or the washing machine for that matter. If either of them is too full, the items will not be fully cleaned as the detergent will not be able to spread as evenly.

Sarah Harding demonstrates how underwear can be worn as outerwear.

Commonly Asked Questions

Q. If I go down a size in my shape wear, will this hold my stomach in even more?

A. No. Wearing a smaller size in shape wear will do nothing other than bring you a great deal of discomfort and grief. Shape wear comes in different control strengths ranging from light to very firm. If you want more control from your shape wear, then all you have to do is look for one with a very strong control level.

Q. How do I stop my bra straps from constantly falling?

A. Women with slanted shoulders will often find that their bra straps are constantly falling down.

Racer-back style bras are a fantastic solution to this problem. If, however, you don't have slanted shoulders and the straps continue to fall even after you have adjusted them, then you are more than likely wearing the wrong size bra.

Q. I have arthritis in my hands and find it difficult to open and close my bra. What kind of bra would you suggest I go for?

A. There are a number of front-fastening bras on the market for women with limited mobility or arthritis. A good lingerie department will be able to provide you with a wide variety.

Lingerie buyer Mary Mullins shares her advice on how women can find the right style to suit them.

Commonly Asked Questions

Q. When briefs are sized as small, medium and large, how do I know which one will best suit my shape?

A. When it comes to finding the right size of underwear, you can still use your dress size as a guide. Women with a dress size of eight are usually an XS, while women of a size ten are classified as a small. Women with a dress size of twelve fall into the medium category while women of a size fourteen or sixteen come under large.

Q. I love the results I get from my shape wear but I hate that I get so hot after just a few hours of wearing it. What can I do?

A. Some shape wear brands can be quite hot, however Rocco is an American brand of shape wear that is growing quite quickly in popularity because its material is so much lighter. Cotton is also beginning to make an appearance in the manufacturing of shape wear garments as it is quite a light breathable fabric.

Q. I'm an A-cup. Is it necessary for me to wear a sports bra when exercising? What is the specific purpose of a sports bra?

A. First of all, you most definitely need to wear a sports bra, regardless of how small your bust is. If your breast ligaments are not adequately supported, the constant motion caused by activities such as exercise will eventually break them down. Sports bras minimise breast movement, thereby minimising damage caused to the ligaments.

Q. Where can I find a strapless bra that won't slip?

A. Finding the right strapless bra that offers adequate support without the risk of slipping can prove a difficult task. Fortunately, Wonderbra have the solution. The Wonderbra Ultimate Strapless Bra was tested for over two years until it was perfected. It has enjoyed phenomenal success since its release and even offers fantastic support for women with large busts.

Discussing the various styles with lingerie buyer Mary Mullins.

LINGERIE DICTIONARY

Babydoll dress

'Babydoll' is the term given to a short dress with cleavage cups and a loose fitting body that falls between the upper thigh and waist. It is usually made from light fabric, such as chiffon or silk, and is often embellished with lace, bows or ribbons.

Balcony bra (also known as balconette bra)

A balcony bra is very similar to the half-cup bra in that it is cut straight across with little or no slant downwards. This style of bra has a corset effect on cleavage and is ideal for giving the bust an enhanced defined shape. A balcony bra is also particularly useful for when you are wearing a scoop neck top and don't want to risk the upper edges of your bra peeking out. If you are naturally big busted, it is best to avoid balcony bras as they will not offer adequate support.

Bandeau bra (also known as tube top)

This is a strapless, wide band worn around the bust line. It is best worn by young women who do not require a good deal of cleavage support.

Basque (also known as bustier)

This is a close-fitting bosom-to-hip bodice that nips the waist to give it a slimmer and more defined shape. Some basques will have detachable straps as well as garter hooks along the lower edge. Basques are often mistakenly referred to as corsets. The main difference between the two garments is that corsets are usually tighter fitting.

Body shaper

A full body shaper is a garment that looks like a one-piece bathing suit. It has control panels to give the body a slimmer and more defined shape. There are a variety of body-shaping garments specific to different parts of the body.

Boy leg brief

This style of brief is reminiscent of hot pants. The waist sits quiet low on the hips, however the back has full coverage. They are best worn under hip-hugger-style trousers or short skirts to give a smooth line from waist to hip.

Boy shorts

Boy shorts are a comfortable form of underwear with a waistband that usually rests on or just below the navel. They provide full back and side coverage and are also very feminine when paired with a camisole and worn as nightwear.

Bralet

A bralet is an unlined, soft cup bra. They are mostly used by teenagers or when sleeping as they do not offer a significant amount of support.

Camisole

A camisole is a light, fitted top with spaghetti straps and can be worn either as underwear or outerwear. Camisoles offer coverage from the bust to the waist but offer very little in terms of breast support. If you don't feel comfortable wearing a cami on its own, you can always wear a bra inside it. This will help give you a nice bust line as well as adequate support.

Chemise

This is a one-piece, loose-hanging garment which was traditionally floor-length. Today, however, it can also refer to a short, sleeveless dress that hangs straight from the shoulders and fits loosely at the waist.

Comfort straps

Comfort straps are usually wider than normal and often have additional padding for extra comfort. They are particularly beneficial for pregnant women or women with a large bust.

Contour bra (also known as T-shirt bra)

A contour bra has moulded cups that hold their shape even when they are not being worn. It gives the bust a beautifully smooth and defined shape and is usually a good option for women with uneven breasts. T-shirt bras are always seamless and have no embellishments. A nude T-shirt bra is the best option when wearing a white top or shirt.

Control brief

This is an item of underwear that is specifically tailored to slim and smooth the midriff area.

Convertible bra (also known as an adjustment bra or multiway bra)

A convertible bra has straps that can be worn in a variety of different ways, for example, halter-neck, one-shoulder, criss-cross and strapless. Convertible bras are not the most comfortable undergarments to wear which is why a lot of women tend to go for the stick on cups rather than fussing with multiway straps. If you want to wear your normal bra with a halter neck top, a good idea is to use a 'multiway converter'. This is basically a clip that holds together the bra straps at the centre of the back so that they won't be seen.

Corset

A corset is a body shaping item of lingerie that is usually boned and tight fitting. It is similar in shape to a basque and is often worn as outerwear usually over a pencil skirt or black pants.

Crossover bra

This is a wire-free bra that overlaps in front to provide additional bust support and comfort.

Gisele promotes the nude contour bra.

Décolleté

This is a very low-cut style of bra that gives the wearer an enhanced cleavage. Décolleté is also the term used to describe a woman's chest area just above her bust line.

Demi-cup bra
(also known as half-cup)

A demi-cup bra is very similar to a balcony bra but not as revealing. A popular style amongst women, it has a contoured shape and is best worn under low necklines.

Full-figure bra

Women who wear bras sizes 32DD and larger are classified as full-figured women. Bras made in these sizes will offer additional support and will usually also feature extra padding, wider shoulder straps and a stronger bra-fastener.

Halter-neck bra

This is a style of bra with straps that fasten behind the neck. It is usually the best option for women who want to wear a bra with a backless dress but who don't want to go strapless.

High-cut brief (also known as French-cut brief)

This item of underwear is cut high at the leg and sides but still offers full coverage at the back.

High-waisted brief

This is the term given to underwear with a high waist that is usually designed to help shape and support the midriff area.

Hipster briefs
(also known as a low-rise brief)

Hipster briefs are usually only worn with low-cut jeans or skirts as they tend to sit on the hip rather than on the waistline like the most briefs.

Hold-ups

This is the term given to stockings that stay up without the aid of garters or a suspender belt. They usually have a silicone band inside the rim to help grip the leg and keep them in place.

Hosiery

This is the collective name given to items such as tights, stockings and socks.

Maternity bra

Specifically designed for women going through pregnancy, this style of bra offers much greater support and comfort. Most maternity bras are designed for breastfeeding and also feature special straps that are designed to reduce bounce when breasts are tender.

Plunge bra

Plunge bras can be bought with or without padding. They are particularly beneficial if you are wearing a low V-neck top as it will give your cleavage a nice shape.

Racer-back bra

A racer-back bra is the perfect solution for any woman who may have sloping shoulders and finds that normal bra straps continuously slip off. The term 'racer-back' essentially means that the garment, whether it be in the form of a T-shirt or a bra, will have straps meeting in a V shape on the back between the shoulder blades. The racer-back style is usually found on sports bras and swimsuits as they tend to offer greater flexibility and movement.

Seamed bra

A seamed bra offers greater support than a seamless bra because the seams that run through the cups determine their exact shape and size.

Seamless bra

A seamless bra is wonderful for giving the wearer a very smooth bust line under a tight fitting top.

Seamless brief

This is a must-have in every woman's wardrobe. They don't leave you at risk of VPL and also give you a slight bum-lift.

Shape wear

This is the term given to a shape-wear garment that not only controls and slims the midriff but also shapes the waist. Contrary to popular belief, shape wear is not all about pulling in the tummy or legs. They also offer wonderful contour and shaping qualities. It's often the case that women just want a certain part of their body to have a nice shape for when they are wearing a dress or an outfit to a special event. When the film and theatre awards season rolls around, you can be sure there isn't one designer gown that doesn't have some form of shape wear hiding underneath it. Eva Longoria and Amanda Holden are just two of many celebrities who have been photographed wearing shape wear.

Waist nipper

A waist nipper is a boned garment that is worn underneath the bust. It extends right down to the waist and is usually fastened at the front with hook-and-eyes. It provides the wearer with a very defined waist as well as a slightly slimmer midriff.

Shoes

When Imelda Marcos and her family were forced to flee the presidential palace in 1986, she left behind almost everything she owned, including a collection for which she had become famous, an astonishing 3,000 pairs of shoes. Not one to be held back, the exuberant former first lady began a new collection and upon her return to the Philippines in 1991, had acquired up to 1,200 pairs of shoes. Within ten years, she had over 1,800 more, bringing her collection to over 3,000 pairs yet again! Talk about dedication!

Then there is the modern day Imelda, aka *Sex and the City*'s Carrie Bradshaw. Remember the famous scene where Carrie is left in a financial dilemma after Aidan moves out and leaves her with just thirty days to buy out his half of the apartment? As she examines her finances, she manages to work out that she has spent $40,000 on shoes over the years. Her classic response? "I will literally be the old woman who lived in her shoes."

Regardless of the arguments that say otherwise, shoes are an integral part of our wardrobe. As well as providing vital protection for our feet every day, a beautiful pair of heels is also a wonderful confidence booster.

It goes without saying that shoes are every bit as integral to the fashion world as the clothes themselves. After all, the right footwear can transform an entire outfit from drab to glam. Unfortunately, a love of shoes can become quite expensive, all is not lost, however! It's a matter or arming yourself with the right advice and shopping sensibly.

Listed below are a variety of pointers and guidelines to help you on your way.

- If a heel breaks or the fabric tears, or even if a strap snaps out of its place, don't immediately assume you have to discard your shoes and buy new ones. Take it to a shoe repair business and see if it can be fixed. Most of the time, the damage is perfectly repairable. For years, I have been advising people to take care of their footwear rather than buying new each time they wear down the sole or break the heel.

- You can't work all day in high heels – it's just not realistic and you will only suffer with bunions in the long run. I personally like to wear insoles so that if I do end up running around in my high heels for a long period of time, at least I know my feet are protected.

- If you're shopping for 'everyday' shoes, or at least shoes that you know you will be wearing regularly, try them on at the end of the day. Your feet expand throughout the day and trying them on in the evening will give you a more accurate sense of whether or not they will fit your feet properly.

- When in two minds over whether or not to buy a particular pair of shoes, ask yourself the following questions: Can I wear these shoes with five or more outfits in my wardrobe? If I buy them, are they likely to be left sitting in their box for the next five months or will I wear them often? Approximately, what is their longevity (for example, are the rhinestones likely to come loose? Is the heel sturdy? Is the fabric likely to get dirty easily?)?

- If you are of heavy build, don't tuck your jeans into your boots as this will only make you appear heavier.

- If your shoes are feeling rather tight, ask your local cobbler to stretch them slightly.

- Put thought into your shoes, even if you're wearing a ball gown. You might assume that no one will notice your footwear underneath a long, flowing gown – but ladies, believe me, if you wear the wrong shoes, people will notice.

- If you are five feet or under, it's always tempting to take on the highest heels possible, but you're far better off staying away from heels that are overly high. They will not flatter your figure. Instead opt for medium-high heels.

- Large platforms with seven-inch heels, straps and lots of detail are fine if being worn under fitted drainpipe jeans or leggings. The same cannot be said for pairing them with dresses,

Christian Louboutin at his 'shoe-signing'.

if you're thinking about buying shoes with a distinctive print, such as snakeskin or leopard skin then you must remember that you will be very limited in what you can wear them with. They will usually only work with two or three looks so try to be conscientious when purchasing.

- Tights worn with open-toe shoes is something I see all the time. I have even seen Kate Moss do it with her Terry de Havilland heels and black opaques. For me, however, it's a big no-no. While it will work with some platform shoes, it won't work if the open toe space is particularly wide and you can see the tights coming through.

however. When wearing a dress, stay away from bulky platforms and instead opt for a more understated shoe.

- There is nothing I dislike more than seeing women wearing white runners underneath beautifully tailored suits. I know women will argue that it makes no sense walking to work in their heels, but white runners are not the only option available. You can now buy pumps that fold up and fit in your handbag. If you're walking a long distance and need pumps with a stronger grip, then look out for 'runner pumps'.

- If you buy shoes that are quite loud and have a lot of colour and diamante embellishment, then you need to treat them as your statement piece and wear them with a very plain outfit. Promote one statement piece only. Likewise,

LISA'S HOME TREATMENTS

To help keep your feet in good condition, it's a good idea to make a chiropodists appointment twice a year. The chiropodist will be able to get rid of any dead skin and afterwards your feet will feel refreshed and revitalised. In the meantime, however, there's an abundance of home treatments you can create to help keep your feet soft and smooth.

Getting rid of tough skin

Before you go to bed, coat your feet with a generous dollop of Vaseline, concentrating particularly on the areas of hard skin, then slip on some cotton socks. When you wake up the following morning, you should notice your feet feel extremely soft.

Relieving foot pain

An age-old remedy for relieving foot pain is to massage coconut oil into the foot, particularly the heel.

Soft feet

After a shower, massage your feet with almond oil to keep them soft and moisturised.

Lemon fresh

Mix together equal amounts of water and lemon juice (approximately half a cup), then dip a washcloth into the mix and apply it to your feet. This will soften and soothe cracked skin on your feet as well as remove any nasty odour-causing bacteria.

Honey feet

Honey is one of the best moisturisers for our skin. To use honey as a foot soother, lather it on and let it sit for fifteen minutes before rinsing off and patting dry. For best results, repeat regularly.

LISA'S TIPS... FOR SHOE CARE

Fresh feet all day

Heat can cause great discomfort, not to mention a nasty odour, in high heels. I know from experience it can also cause painful blisters. To avoid the risk of encountering any of these side effects, shake a little talcum powder into your shoes and it will prevent the build up of heat from occurring throughout the day.

"You put high heels on and you change."
Manolo Blahnik

Shoe too tight?

Thanks to this tip, you will never again have to endure the discomfort of a tight fitting leather shoe. Put a few drops of water into the toe of the shoe and wear them around the house for fifteen to twenty minutes. When the water combines with the heat from your foot, it will help the leather soften and expand around your toes. If you would rather not wet them, then use a hot hairdryer instead.

Reviving those old suede shoes

If a stain appears on your suede shoes or if they are looking a bit dull from constant wear, rub them very gently with an emery board. Afterwards, hold the shoe over the steam rising from a bowl of boiling water or a kettle. This will remove the stain.

High heel know-how

- Six-inch heels (and higher) may seem like a tempting purchase, unfortunately, they can usually only be worn by women with a shoe size larger than a size six or seven, otherwise you risk damaging your feet. If you are wearing heels that are too high, your toes will be left carrying the bulk of your weight. This can result in severe damage, particularly if the toe of the shoe is also pointed or tight. Surgery may even be required to correct the resulting problems.

- If the ball of your foot does not touch the floor when you walk, then take it as a sign that the heels are too high for your foot and so shouldn't be worn. A good way of finding out if your new shoes are too high is to stand in your heels with your knees straight and see if you can raise yourself up on your toes by about an inch. If you can't, your heels are too high!

- We've all experienced that burning feeling in our feet during a night of dancing. While it might be tempting to kick off your shoes for a few minutes, this is actually a big mistake! Your feet will swell slightly after you take off your shoes, which, in turn, will make it even more uncomfortable when you slip them back on. To minimise high-heel-induced foot pain on a night out, wear cushioned inserts.

- When walking in high heels, always take short steps rather than long strides.

- If you're not used to wearing high heels but would like to start, then don't jump in at the deep end and buy a pair of stilettos. It's essential that you first train your feet to footwear of a new height, particularly if you have been living in flats. Begin by wearing shoes with a low heel or, better still, wedge heels of a medium height. When you become accustomed to wearing these, progress to shoes that are slightly higher. By taking things gradually, you will find that you are so much more confident when it comes to walking in heels of a trickier height.

- It's always a good idea to wear new shoes around the house before you wear them out as this will scuff the heels very slightly thereby making them less slippery. When breaking in new shoes, make sure you wear them outside your house as well as inside. Walking on hard ground such as tarmac will help prepare your feet for when you really wear your heels out.

"I was born in high heels and I've worn them ever since."

Helena Christensen

Queen of heels, Tamara Mellon president and co-founder of Jimmy Choo shoes.

"Give a girl the right pair of shoes and she can conquer the world."

Every time I see this quotation, Irish shoe designer Nina Divito, immediately spring's to mind. She is without doubt the perfect example of someone who has worked hard to transfer her dream from the sketchpad to the shop floor.

In a bid to help fund her debut shoe collection, Nina began painting pictures of shoes and selling them through exhibitions. Such was the success of her painting, that her work is still being commissioned. Today, the beautiful shoe designs that were once confined to canvas, are being made in Italy by the very people who make footwear for Louis Vuitton and Gucci.

For anyone, this would be the ultimate dream realised, but Nina is not just anyone. Ambitious, determined and persistent, she has an endless supply of big ideas. What's more she has even bigger plans to make them a reality!

"Tough Days. There will be many moments like this – small anxieties, delays, nuisances but one day soon, you will open a beautiful black and white box, roll back the tissue, smell the richness of the leather and take out your first pair of shoes! It will happen... and you know it will."

Q. Nina, where did your dream begin?

A. To be completely honest, I never saw myself as an artist. I love painting but as a craft, I never felt it was my thing. I viewed it as a way of expressing myself. I really dreaded exhibitions because when it came to the art world, I never felt as though I fitted in. I didn't have the confidence to believe that I was a good painter and that I deserved to be there. Instead I just thought, Oh my god, what am I doing here?

I remember meeting the artist Rasher and I was in complete awe of him; he was so lovely and inspiring. One of the things he said to me was that there's a place for everyone in the art world and that my technique didn't have to match Picasso or Monet in order for me to be accepted as an artist. He was just so encouraging.

The one thing that kept me motivated in my painting was my end goal of being a shoe designer. I saw painting as a platform to get my designs out there; a way of obtaining a reaction to the shoes before they were made so that I could see if people liked them as much as I did. When my work received a very good reaction, it was an amazing injection of confidence because it made me realise that it wasn't just me who liked the designs.

I then went on to work for Olivia Morris in London for six months. It was like an internship and I absolutely loved it, but it got to the stage where I had to return home. It was at that point that I started sending out CVs. I was so eager to get a step in the door of the design world that I would have gladly taken a job sweeping floors, anything to just get me in there. Often I wouldn't even get a reply. There were so many days when I just thought, Why am I doing this?, and, of course, there were times when I felt so down because it seemed like I wasn't getting anywhere with it. In a way, the painting kept me going because I would suddenly think of an amazing idea for a design and I would work on it for the following month. It was a wonderful distraction. I try not to go anywhere without a sketchbook so that whenever an idea hits me, I can just jot it down and return to it later when I have time.

Q. Did you find rejection hard or did it encourage you to keep going?

A. I would encounter knock-backs, but then I'd wake up the following morning and find that the knock-back would have made me even more determined to succeed! I remember when Manolo Blahnik held a launch in Brown Thomas in Dublin, I just stood at the opposite side of the room, looking at him. He had such an incredible presence. One of the PR girls suggested that I go up and meet him, but I was so star struck that I didn't feel as though I'd be able to say anything to him. Two minutes later, the PR girl marched me up to him and introduced me. She told him that I painted shoes and instantly he began asking me about it. All that went through my head was, Oh my God, he's talking to me!

I told him about my aspirations to be a shoe designer and he was so encouraging. He kept saying, "Do it! You have to do it!" He then gave me brilliant advice about how to approach people within the industry. He told me not to waste my time phoning or writing but instead to travel to Italy and knock on doors. He explained that's how he got started. That night, I was thinking what what he had said to me and I realised that he was absolutely right. By that stage, I had lost count of the amount of phone calls I had made and the amount of emails and letters I had sent. The Italians are hilarious because they'll just hang up on you without any warning! There was also the issue of the language barrier because I don't speak Italian, so I really felt that the only way to get a foot in the door was to take Manolo Blahnik's advice and just go over there and meet them face to face.

Q. I'm getting goosebumps just thinking about your conversation with Manolo Blahnik! What did you do next?

A. One day, I was exhibiting my paintings at a trade fair and the woman whose stand was next to mine was a jewellery designer called Rebecca Davis. We got chatting and she suggested that I contact Eddie Shanahan, whom she said had been so helpful to her in the early stages of her career. That night, I composed an email to send to him. In it, I outlined who I was and the goal I was trying to achieve with my designs. The following Saturday morning, I received a reply in which he basically said he would be happy to help me. My mother isn't big into fashion but when I mentioned Eddie's name to her she immediately knew who he was and what he did. His reputation was just so strong. I arranged to meet him and, during our meeting, I showed him the designs for the collection.

Q. What was his initial reaction to your designs?

A. When Eddie reached the fourth page, he knew I was serious about it. I remember being so nervous prior to the meeting because these were designs that I had never before shown anyone. I loved that he instinctively knew it was going to be a luxury collection and I distinctly remember him saying to me, "You want to compete with Jimmy Choo, Chanel and Louboutin." In my heart, I felt that my shoes were just as good as those designers but I always felt uneasy about saying it openly.

Eddie told me that he wanted to take me to Italy the following week to meet influential people in the business but that he wouldn't do so until I could stand up and admit that my shoes were just as good if not better than the high-end designers. It took me such a long time to admit it, but it wasn't until I met Eddie that I was able to say it out loud.

The following week, we travelled to Italy where we visited a number of factories. The third factory we called to was run by a husband and wife and the second I got there, I just knew it was the place where I wanted my shoes to be made. I can't explain how I knew — we didn't even speak the same language — but I just had this good feeling about it. I showed them my portfolio and when the owner was a few pages in, he suddenly started shouting in Italian. My heart sank; I was so convinced we were going to be thrown out. There was another man at the meeting called Gorgio, who is now my agent in Italy, and he was translating for us. While the man was shouting, Georgio was sitting there smiling. I asked him what the man was saying and Georgio just replied, "This is great! He's shouting that we're in the wrong place and that he has to bring us to where they make shoes for Louis Vuitton and Jimmy Choo!" I don't think I have ever been so shocked!

Q. That's such a remarkable achievement! Do you get to work with the shoemakers?

A. I love being in the factory and working with the craftsmen. I trained in shoemaking, so, for me, there's nothing like sitting down with a seventy-year-old Italian shoemaker who has been in the trade all his life. I learn so much from it. I absolutely love the whole process of creating shoes, discussing the design with the craftsman and feeling the different materials that will be used. Sometimes, we have our arguments but even though at the time I worry that I was out of order to insist on something like a more expensive material or a natural fibre, it's when I see the collection that I know I was right to stick to my guns.

When I tried on my shoes for the first time, it was such an amazing feeling. The one thing I was adamant about from the start was that my shoes were not to be seasonal. I want women to be able to wear my shoes all year round.

Q. What inspires ideas for new designs?

A. When I sit down to design a shoe, I try to envision the kind of shoe that everyone wants, but that no one has yet managed to get. Primarily, that's what inspires my designs. It's much more exciting that way.

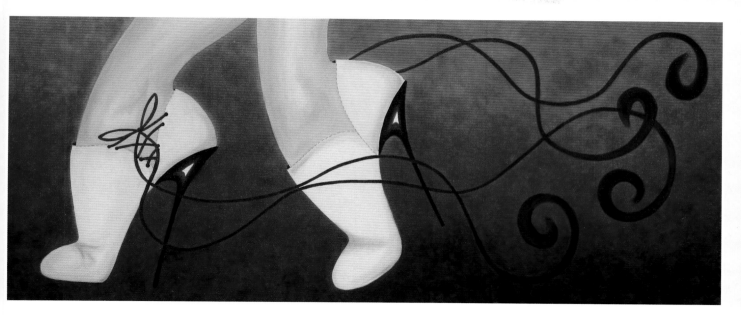

Q. What is your favourite part of the process?

A. I love the creative side of things, but I find the business side so daunting! Before I began painting, I had no idea what a press release was or how PR worked. It acted as a starting point and a great training ground on how to do interviews and deal with press. The publicity I received from my paintings prepared me for the publicity I now receive for my shoe collection. It also helped build my brand in a way.

I had been painting for seven or eight years, so my first collection of shoes was definitely very special for me. After I designed the first collection, I decided to name a shoe after each person who had helped me along the way or who had been an inspiration to me. I gave the name Eddie to the nappa leather court shoe which has organdy rose detail and thorns around the heel. For some reason that shoe gets so much press! Whenever Eddie is asked about why the shoe was named after

him, he jokes that it relates to the phrase 'thorn in my side'!

My painting of the Eddie shoe was actually one of my most popular paintings, so it's nice that it's now also one of my bestselling shoes.

Q. How do you decide on the height of a heel for a shoe?

A. A normal height for a heel is five inches. I always wanted my signature shoes to be five inches but my mum wanted me to design shoes with a lower heel as well, so I decided to include a three-inch heel, which she loves. My younger sister on the other hand wanted a higher heel so, for the next season, I have created a shoe with a six-inch heel!

When designing my collection, huge emphasis and work goes into the quality and comfort of the shoes. For years, I suffered in beautiful shoes. A couple of hours wearing them and I would get that burning sensation in the balls of my feet. After a few more hours, I'd have to retire to my seat as I couldn't bear the pain any longer! It's because of this that I understand the importance of comfort in a shoe. As such I spend a huge amount of time making sure my shoes are every bit as comfortable as they are beautiful. I source the softest nappa leathers, spend months searching for the right shock-absorbing platforms, put in extra padding where needed

and literally spend most of my time running up and down the stairs in the factory going, "Not quite right, Andrea… nearly there… just need to make them slightly softer." I'm sure I drive them mad, but I just feel it's such a sin to leave a beautiful pair of shoes in the wardrobe. They must be worn, therefore they must be comfortable.

Q. You're so passionate and determined to see your dream realised.

A. I suppose I have always been very passionate about my shoes. The factory where my shoes are made is also responsible for making shoes for brands such as Gucci and Yves St Laurent and, at one point, they admitted they didn't need my brand because they already had enough to work on. However, they said they could sense I was very passionate about my work and that I wasn't going to go away any time soon!

Nina's tips on caring for your shoes

- Listen to your common sense. If you buy a pair of cream satin shoes, it doesn't matter how expensive they were or what designer made them, they will not survive muck and rain, so don't wear them to the races!

- Get the heels repaired before they are worn down to the point where you can see and hear the iron in the heel as you walk. Driving in shoes will also scuff the heels, so try to wear pumps when behind the wheel.

- If you find that the heels of your shoes are caving inwards, it's because the shanks and the structure of the shoes are not strong enough. This shouldn't

happen with good-quality shoes, but, if it does, you need to watch how you are walking as it could be the reason why the heels are caving inwards. You should also bring them to a cobbler and see if they can be restored.

Accessories

I love encouraging women to look at using their accessories in various innovative ways. I have lived in the same clothes for years but people wouldn't know it because I have worn them in so many different ways. I tweak them to create different looks.

SCARVES

Most women see the humble scarf as a form of neck-wear or head-covering but I see it as the perfect way to inject new life into a stale look – what better way to transform a plain dull bag than to attach a trendy scarf to the handles?

If you want to add a unique touch to a plain hairstyle such as a ponytail, why not wrap a scarf around the hair-tie? Rather than using a belt with your jeans, try slipping a scarf through the loops for a more individual touch.

When it comes to accessories, forget the boundaries and use your imagination. Be as creative as possible by playing around with different items to see what new looks you can create. When you start doing this, you will quickly develop an eye for finding just the right accessories to complement your look.

"Accessories are what, in my opinion, pull the whole look together and make it unique."

Yves St Laurent

Elle MacPherson uses a scarf to give her clutch bag an element of style.

SHAWLS

A lot of women dislike their arms and think they are too flabby. There are two things they can do when approaching this problem: either exercise or cover them up. Shawls and long-sleeved shrugs are perfect for the second option. What's more, there's wonderful variety in the different ways in which you can wear the style.

Cape

To create the cape look, rest the shawl on your shoulders and let the ends hang down in front. Next tie the ends in a knot thereby creating the style of a capelet.

Wrap

For the wrap, drape the shawl over the shoulders. Next bring the entire width of both ends to cross over in front of you before tying them together at the back.

Grace Kelly

Drape the shawl over your shoulders before taking the end of the left side and throwing it over the right shoulder. To keep it in place, pin it with a broach or safety pin, hidden underneath the shoulder of the shawl.

Shawl top

A great way to wear a long shawl with a white shirt or tank top is to drape it around your neck, allow it to hang down in front, then place a belt around your waist and over the scarf. Just make sure the colours work well together.

Urban chic

To try out this style, you will need two light shawls of two different colours. Gently entwine them before draping them around your neck.

Skirt/Sarong

You can easily turn a light shawl into a sarong. Just wrap it around your waist and secure properly with a knot or a clip. It looks great when casually paired with jeans or leggings. Remember, this look won't work with all shawls so choose carefully.

HATS

1. Trilby
2. Baker Boy
3. Beanie
4. Beret
5. Wide brimmed hat

Years ago, if you wanted to get ahead, you got yourself a hat!

Even though hats are very much back in fashion, we still have a tendency to associate them with special events such as weddings or the races. The reality, however, is that hats can be worn any where, any time! It's all about finding the right one!

To achieve a casual chic look, trilby hats and baker boy caps are ideal. For upscale elegance, berets make for a stylish accessory. On the other hand, if you want a very casual style, there's a wide range of beanie hats to enjoy!

However, in order to choose the right hat, there are a number of points you will need to keep in mind.

- **Fashion hindrance or fashion statement?**
  You want to be completely comfortable in your hat, but this will prove impossible if your hat is quite big and constantly brushing against those standing next to you. This will make you very self-conscious and you will find it very difficult to relax as a result. Before you buy, ask yourself if the headwear in question is appropriate for the event and venue or if it will end up being more of a fashion hindrance than a fashion statement.

- **Hair know-how**
  If you're wearing a clip-in headpiece to a wedding ceremony and plan to take it off after the ceremony, make sure you ask your hairdresser how you can do so without ruining your upstyle.

- **Headwear versus eyewear**
  If you wear glasses, make sure they don't detract from your hat, otherwise the look may appear very busy. One should complement the other. If you have your heart set on a particular hat but find it doesn't work with your eyewear, then why not consider wearing contact lenses that day.

Proportion

The hat must match the proportion of your face. If you have a square jaw line, soften the face with a round hat. If you have a round face, look for a hat that has a sharper edge and a more defined square style.

The size of your face will also be a factor in the style of hat that will flatter your frame. If your face is quite small, opt for a relatively small hat, otherwise is the hat will overwhelm your face. If you have a wide face, go for a hat with a wide brim as a small hat will only make your face appear wider.

Complexion

It's vital that the colour of your hat complements your skin tone particularly if you are wearing a trilby hat, a wide-brimmed hat or baker boy cap. As these styles sit very close to the face, the wrong colour could leave your complexion looking tired and drained. The right colour, however, will add to your face and leave you looking healthy and bright. If you want to start with a safe colour but find that black looks too heavy, then try navy, crimson, dark purple or dark brown. As you become more accustomed to your new accessory, you will find it so much easier to be creative with colours.

Sarah Jessica Parker gets it right.

Body size

If you are of short stature, opt for hats that have height on top, such as trilbys. It's also a good idea to go for a hat that has one solid colour rather than a hat with patterns as busy styles will make you appear shorter. Wide hats can work on petite women but only as long as they're not so wide they appear too big for your head! Keep it in proportion!

If you have a tall frame, look for hats that have a wide brim. Hats that have patterns will also complement your height without making you appear taller. If you're a plus size, avoid small hats and patterned styles as these will not flatter your frame. If anything they will only make you appear larger.

Accessorise

Give your trilby or beret a unique touch by securing a broach to the side of the hat front. To brighten up a trilby, attach a ribbon.

Outfit

When it comes to attaining causal chic, your hat should pull the whole outfit together rather than stand out on its own. Of course, if you're attending an event and want the hat to be your statement piece, it's perfectly fine for it to stand out, just make sure you tone down other accessories. Remember, casual chic can take you anywhere because it is what it says – causal yet chic. I once attended a fashion show where one of the guests was wearing high-waisted grey trousers with a plain white tank top and a grey trilby hat. She was easily one of the best-dressed people there. If ever you are worried about being over dressed at an event, go for the causal chic look and you can't go wrong.

Angles

Experiment with your hat; position it at different angles to see which is most flattering. Avoid pushing it to the back of your head as this is not a particularly nice look. Tilting it to the side, however, is usually fail safe.

Inspiration

If you are looking for inspiration on how to wear different hats (or indeed if you want to discover the range of hats you could be wearing) hit the internet and study the styles worn by icons such as Ava Gardner, Marilyn Monroe, Debbie Harry, Grace Kelly and Brigitte Bardot. Remember, history determines the styles of today!

Brigitte Bardot

Sunglasses

- Oversized sunglasses will not work if you have very high cheekbones. They will mark your face and leave a line which will take hours to get rid of. If you want to invest in a good pair of sunglasses, pay a visit to a reputable eyewear shop and ask the assistant to fit you with sunglasses.

- A quick way to find out if a pair of sunglasses are right for your face is to sit them on your nose. If you cannot see out over them, they are not the right shape for you.

- Some people love sunglasses with lots of crystal detail on the sides. If you fall into this category then you need to remember one rule – no earrings. You should not wear earrings if your sunglasses already have embellishments on the side. The key is simplicity. If you're buying sunglasses with colourful frames, then you need to remember you will be very limited in terms of both clothes and jewellery. This is why black frames are always the best option as they will go with absolutely everything.

- Some people find that their sunglasses mark the bridge of their nose when they take them off. If your glasses fit you properly, however, they won't leave any marks.

- When it comes to sunglasses, it's not about the size of your face, it's about the shape. For instance, a round pair of sunglasses will not suit a round face as it will only make the face look fuller.

- When sunglasses are too big, they 'sit' on your face and, because of this, they end up hurting you. They will also cause you annoyance because they will move up and down every time you talk or smile. Sunglasses should always be resting just above the cheek.

Audrey Hepburn

Sunglasses

- The level of UV protection in sunglasses is something you need to query before you buy. With some glasses, even a scratch can damage the UV filter and, as a result, this magnifies the UV rays being exposed to your eyes. There are exceptions however. Okli branded sunglasses for instance are made for extreme sports and are designed in a way that scratches won't damage the UV filter.

- When caring for your sunglasses, never use tissue to wipe away any smudges or dirt as it will only drag the dirt across the lens, causing it to scratch. Don't worry if you have lost the little cloth that comes with your glasses, you can always buy micro fibre cloths and special silicone-based sprays for cleaning them. It is always a good idea to buy the correct products for cleaning the lenses as anything else will only spread the dirt across the lens rather than lifting it.

- If those tiny screws in your frames keep loosening, try coating them with a light layer of clear nail polish. This will secure them in place but won't prevent them from being removed if this becomes necessary. Just make sure you don't get any nail varnish on the lenses.

- If the plastic arms of your sunglasses are slightly out of shape, then blast them with a hairdryer or hold them over a hot radiator. Once the heat makes the plastic slightly flexible, shape them back in place.

Top Tip

If you're worried that you have over-accessorised and can't decide which item to remove, try the following tip. Turn your back to the mirror and then quickly turn around and look at your reflection. Take off the first accessory you see!

BELTS

Is it just me or are belts getting more and more decorative by the season?

For as long as I can remember, I have always been a huge fan of belts as I feel they really complete an outfit. From the plain to the embellished, I've worn them all! Unfortunately, quite a lot of women avoid belts as they are conscious of them highlighting a troublesome midriff area. What they don't realise, however, is that the right belt can actually slim the appearance.

It's all about how you wear it!

"Accessories are important and becoming more and more important every day."

Giorgio Armani

- How you position your belt can make or break your look. Don't assume the belt must always sit on your waist. In fact, this can sometimes be the worst place for it. Stand in front of a mirror and see what works for your body shape. Maybe sit the belt just below your waist, or perhaps bring it up underneath your bust to create an empire waist. Try them all – it's the only way to determine which belt-position will work best for your shape!

- When choosing a belt, make sure it is appropriate for your size. For instance, if you are carrying a little extra weight around the stomach area, then avoid wearing ultra-thin belts. These will only highlight the area by giving you the dreaded muffin top. Instead, opt for a wide belt and position it at the thinnest part of your waist. It will cinch the area in question, thereby giving you the appearance of a smaller waist. This is also a good tip if you are quite thin and want to emphasise your waist without having to wear a corset.

- If you're petite, steer clear of belts as they will make you appear shorter in height.

- Make sure you jewellery matches the colour of your belt, so if your belt is silver, make sure your jewellery corresponds with the colour theme. Some people will argue that it's ok to mix silver and gold items but I think women look much better when they stick to either one or the other.

- A belt can totally transform a dress. Remember, if the dress is glamorous, the belt should be plain.

Katherine Jenkins adds a feminine touch to her patterned dress with a plain ribbon belt…

…when wearing a plain dress however, she injects a touch of glamour with a patterned ribbon belt.

- Opt for dark-coloured belts if you are conscious of your midriff as these will slim the appearance of your torso.

- If comfort is your main requirement from a belt, then look for belts with strong elasticity.

COSTUME JEWELLERY

Jackie Kennedy

Pearls, pearls, pearls

Remember Jackie Kennedy's pearls? They're practically fashion legend, but little did people know at the time they were fake! If you can't afford real pearls, browse around accessory shops for costume jewellery pearls that look identical to the real thing. It's my firm belief that unless you're a jewellery connoisseur, only the woman wearing the pearls knows whether they are real or fake. Jackie Kennedy is testament to this!

- If you are attending a formal event and want to give your outfit an added touch of elegance, follow in the footsteps of icons such as Coco Chanel and Princess Diana and let your pearls rest on your back!

- If you want to add your own individual touch to a long string of pearls, attach a broach or flower midway. Experiment!

- You don't have to wear pearls on their own. For a very modern look, wear your pearls with other necklaces. Just make sure the top you are wearing them with is quite plain. Remember, the statement is being made by the jewellery.

- Before wearing your pearls, look at your outfit in its entirety and ask yourself if they would look better hanging loose or wrapped around your neck as a choker.

- Your jewellery should be the last items you put on and the first items you take off. Products such as perfumes, deodorants, moisturisers and even make-up can all contribute to the discolouration and tarnishing of jewellery.

- Moisture is the enemy of jewellery as it can damage the surface and cause rust. When cleaning your jewellery, always ensure that you dry it thoroughly. If you have been wearing jewellery in particularly hot weather, before you store it away make sure you gently rinse the items with water before patting them dry with a soft cloth as perspiration can greatly shorten the life of jewellery. Do not use tissue as the particles may scratch the surface.

- Never use soap when cleaning jewellery as it can sometimes leave a residue that causes stones and surfaces to appear dull. Old wives tales suggest using vinegar to give jewellery a shine but this is ill-advised as vinegar can be quite harmful to certain materials, particularly gemstones.

- Never leave your jewellery sitting in the sunlight. A dramatic change of temperature can affect the glue used in the embellishments.

- Buy an extra-soft child's toothbrush to use for when thoroughly cleaning your items of jewellery. The bristles are ideal for accessing those hard-to-reach places.

- Hang up your pearls and necklaces rather than boxing them away.

- A lot of women assume their jewellery must match the colour of the top or dress they are wearing. This is completely untrue. If anything, contrasting colours will compliment your outfit and make it stand out even more.

- When buying diamante jewellery, always remember the bigger the diamond the more fake it will look.

- If you have a long face, avoid wearing long droopy earrings. This particular style only suits women who wish to add length to their face. Long earrings are also good for slimming a round face. When wearing an elaborate style of earring, highlight it by wearing your hair in an upstyle. For greater effect however, wear a V-neck or strapless top. On that note, never make the mistake of combining a dramatic necklace with elaborate earrings. Choose one statement piece only. If your necklace is detailed, then make sure your earrings are plain, and vice versa.

- Coco Chanel long maintained that you should always remove the last accessory you put on. Feng Shui, likewise, states that wearing too much jewellery can lead to an imbalance of energy. Again, the age-old adage rings true – less is definitely more.

- If you like the trend of wearing multiple bangles on one hand, then keep your other jewellery very simple. Your bangles are the statement piece and, therefore, should not be overwhelmed by other jewellery items, such as loud necklaces. Some years ago, I went through a bling phase and I look back now and think I must have looked like a Las Vegas showgirl!

- Never store silver with other metals, otherwise it will tarnish.

Beyoncé allows her earrings make the statement by simplifying the rest of her ensemble.

- If you are wearing patterns, make sure your jewellery is very simple. You want to achieve a look that is balanced rather than busy.

- Steer clear of short necklaces if you have a very round face or a double chin. Long necklaces on the other hand are a great solution as they will draw the eye away from the facial area. They are also good for people who are petite and want to create the illusion of an elongated frame. If, however, you have a very long neck, try wearing medium- to short-length jewellery.

- When wearing a top with a turtleneck, always pair it with long necklaces. Short pendants will not look right.

LISA'S TIPS... FOR COSTUME JEWELLERY

No more green jewellery lines

Inexpensive costume jewellery can sometimes leave an unsightly green stain on your skin. To prevent this from happening, paint the inside of the jewellery with some clear nail varnish and allow it to dry. The next time you wear it, your skin won't be tarnished.

Stuck ring

It has happened to us all. We try on a beautiful ring only to find it is suddenly stuck and unwilling to move. Instead of reaching for the margarine, reach for the hair conditioner. Rub some hair conditioner on your finger and the ring should slide right off. Lip balm is also wonderful for helping to remove stuck rings.

Pearly shine

Pearl buttons and embellishments will keep their shine for longer if you paint them with a light coat of clear nail varnish.

Injection of sparkle

If a piece of costume jewellery has lost its sparkle then try dropping it in a cup of water with some fizzing Alka-Seltzer tablets. This tip is brilliant for reviving dull-looking jewellery pieces and leaves them with a new clean shine.

ACCESSORISING A BUSINESS SUIT

"We've come a long way. Power dressing now is designed to let the woman inside us come through."
Donna Karan

Why is it we always associate black suits with the business world? There is such a remarkable range of sharp vibrant styles out there that women no longer need to resign their business wardrobe solely to dull shades and styles.

While I agree that every woman should own a sharp black suit, I do think it's nice to vary your look and have other options to choose from.

For inspiration, take a look at Victoria Beckham's designs. The sharp edge that makes her dresses so distinctive is perfect for a corporate environment. Fortunately, the high street has introduced a plethora of dresses in a similar style to those created by Mrs Beckham and, what's more, they can usually be found in a range of elegant colours. If all else fails, look back at the styles boasted by the icons and take your inspiration from the classics. Remember Marlene Dietrich's crisp white ruffled shirt and sharp black trousers? Ideal for the office!

Play around with the basics of your wardrobe and see what looks you can devise. If, however, you still feel that your professional style requires an injection of joie-de-vivre, then look to your collection of accessories for help! Below is a list of guidelines to help you on your way.

- When choosing a bracelet to wear, think ahead and ask yourself if it will obstruct your use of the computer keyboard. Charm bracelets may be beautiful but they can be as equally annoying when you're trying to type.

- Don't forget the range of elegant items available for your hair, such as jewelled barrettes and dressage hair bun holders. Even a simple thin black ribbon tied in a bow at the nape of a hair bun will bring an added touch of class to your appearance. The key is to keep the overall look elegant and neat.

- When wearing jewellery with a business suit, less is so much more. Choose just two items (three at most) from the following list: diamond or pearl bracelet, delicate necklace, simple earrings such as pearl or diamond studs, or an understated ring. A corporate environment is no place for loud dramatic costume jewellery such as bangles and large rings. If you really want to liven up a plain suit with a colourful accessory, wear a neck scarf.

- If you don't like wearing jewellery, keep an eye out for elegant broaches to pin to your suit jacket. Broaches look particularly well with skirt suits.

- Always wear a watch as it symbolises punctuality, but only ever wear neat classic styles. Watches with plastic straps or loud bright colours are not appropriate for the workplace.

- Belts are fantastic for transforming the look of an entire outfit. If you're wearing black, try pairing it with a belt in a contrasting colour such as crimson or purple.

- Shawls, of course, are wonderfully elegant. You can pair pretty much any colour with a white shirt over black trousers. If you don't want to wear a shawl, however, wear a neck scarf.

ACCESSORISING A LITTLE BLACK DRESS (LBD)

Accessorising your LBD with a long-sleeved shrug

A wonderful way to add instant colour to your LBD is to pair it with a bright, long-sleeved shrug. As you can see in this demonstration, I chose an elegant red shrug.

| Take one end of the shrug, bring it across the torso and up over the shoulder. To keep it in place, secure it with a broach. | Take both ends of the shrug and cross them over each other before securing them loosely at the sides with a pin. | Bring the ends of the shrug underneath your arms before tying them at the back. This will give you a bolero-style shrug. | Take one end of the shrug, bring it across the torso. Next, take the other end, bring it across your torso over the other shrug end and up onto your shoulder. | Tie the shrug at the front, allowing the ends to hang down. | If all else fails, just let it hang down loosely! |

There are so many different ways in which you can add your own unique touch to a LBD. To create a very elegant look, pin an eye-catching broach to the top corner of the dress. There is an abundance of beautiful, inexpensive broaches available from accessory shops so you should have no trouble finding the right one for your dress. On the other hand, you could cinch the waist with a belt. If the belt is quite large or detailed, then treat it as the statement piece and tone down your jewellery.

If you're in a business environment, then pair the dress with a long black coat. Keep the look sharp and professional.

For a night out, wear your LBD with a military jacket, high heels/ankle boots and a costume necklace. If you are wearing the dress to a formal event, such as a wedding, combine it with dramatic elegant jewellery or a statement hairpiece. Bring along a shawl if you're worried about feeling the cold. Just make sure it works with the colour of your accessories.

Adjust the dress to suit your individual preferences. If you don't like baring your neck and shoulders, then drape a shawl across the neck area before gently bringing one of the ends up and over the shoulders. Take a look at page 94 to find out the several different ways in which you can change an entire outfit with a simple shawl. If you don't want to wear a shawl, try pairing it with a slim fitting jacket.

If you're self-conscious about your legs, wear opaque tights. The LBD works for everyone, it's just a matter of establishing what works for you.

Always be on the lookout for different styles of LBDs. There are so many different designs available, it's just a matter of seeking them out. If you already own a LBD and love its fit and shape then enquire with the retailer if the same designer has brought out new versions of the dress. It's often the case a designer will reintroduce the original design after having tweaked and improved it.

KAREN MILLEN, DESIGNER

Karen Millen's creations are like architecture for the body. Sharp fluid styles that remain true to femininity, her designs have become synonymous with elegance. Ever since she introduced her creations to the world back in 1981, Karen's hard work and optimistic attitude have made her a force in the fashion industry. What's more, she is a genuinely nice person. No airs, graces or diva tantrums, she is the epitome of class. Fortunately for her fans, Karen has now turned her creative talents to interior design. I recently chatted with the iconic designer about everything from style tips to wearing Shirley Bassey's gowns!

Q. Karen, I read that you started off with a loan of just £100 which you used to begin manufacturing and selling white shirts to your friends. It's never easy starting up a new venture so can you recall how you remained optimistic, motivated and upbeat throughout the tough times?

A. I have always been a very positive person. I guess having such a passion for what I was doing and a belief in what we had to offer kept us going through those difficult periods. I believe we all have to undergo bad experiences to understand the rights and wrongs, the good and the bad, to test our strengths and weaknesses. Life is full of challenges and no success comes without tough experiences.

Q. I read that your mother inspired your love of fashion. Can you tell us more about the ways in which she inspired you?

A. I wouldn't say she inspired my love of fashion as she wasn't particularly in tune with it and still isn't! What she did do was make clothes for my sister and I, probably through lack of money, and she also used to knit a lot so I became more interested in fashion and I would challenge her to make me clothes. She even made me a coat one year because I couldn't find a fashionable one in my size at the time. My passion for fashion was something I just seemed to have adopted from an early age and developed over the years.

Q. There are always a few items that never appear to go out of style. Can you share with us the items and accessories that you believe are trend resistant?

A. Without sounding too cliché, the black dress has to be up there. I have a Gucci one which I must have had now for at least fifteen years. The fabric is a dense thick silk with a slight sheen, and the cut and shape is amazing. I still wear it to this day. It's something that is totally timeless and whenever I have a moment when every other dress looks awful, I take this one out and I don't even have to think about if it will work.

I am always in possession of a black tailored jacket or two. Again, tailoring has been key to my look and although trends on tailoring come and go, I would always have a favourite to wear when the time seems fitting. Jeans have been an important part of my wardrobe for many years now. Bags are also my big accessory love. Along with fashion pieces I do try to buy carefully in terms of investment pieces. These tend to perhaps be the less obvious must-have bags, but rather something more timeless and obscure. I love nothing more than pulling out an old piece that still works really well today and knowing that not many others would be carrying the same! It just injects your look with a touch of individuality.

Q. Are there any items in your wardrobe that you would never part with or that have interesting stories behind them?

A. There are a lot of items in my wardrobe that I wouldn't part with. I try to buy well and I love to take the clothes back out when the time feels right. Although just lately I have been feeling like I need to let go of some of the clothes that I know I won't ever wear again. I do however have two very interesting pieces in my wardrobe. They are two outfits that I bought at a Christie's auction – Shirley Bassey stage costumes worn in the 1960s complete with capes and shoes! One is a beaded and sequined dress in an ivory colour, full length, very timeless and stunning. I have worn it on a couple of occasions and, funnily enough, when I wore it to Elton John's White Tie and Tiara Ball a few years ago, I ended up being seated at the same table as Shirley Bassey herself! Very bizarre! Not sure how she felt about me wearing the dress but she was in a great mood and we enjoyed a glass of champagne together. The other item is a taupe silk catsuit embellished with turquoise beads. It's very 1960s, very cool and I have already worn it on a couple of occasions. I love them both and would never part with them.

Q. What tips could you offer to women who want their work-wear to look stylish yet professional? How can they make sure their outfit is stylish yet suitable for the office?

A. Keep it simple, fairly classic with perhaps a few current accessories to keep it on trend. You need to feel comfortable and not like you are trying too hard. Make it a rule to wear the clothes and not allow them to wear you.

Q. You have stated in the past that you like to take the positive from a negative experience. In the book, we cover the benefits of positive thinking. Can you explain why a positive outlook is important to you?

A. Being positive is what drives me every day; it's what gives me my energy. Time is too precious to be negative and although at times it's hard to stay positive, when I have those down days I know they are just temporary and that I have to allow myself to have them as long they are just short term. Perhaps as you get older and have lived more of life's experiences that you realise there is no time to waste on negativity. Negativity is like a poison that gets into the system and destroys people. It's such a waste.

Q. Can you tell us about your involvement in HOPE-HIV and the Gateway School of Fashion?

A. I have spent time working alongside a charity called HOPE-HIV at setting up a school for young people affected by the HIV pandemic in South Africa. This course ran for two years in which time we trained thirty-seven young people in skills in fashion giving them the tools to become self-sufficient, independent and hopeful for a better future. Unfortunately, funding has run out and although the school is in operation, it is focusing on general sewing skills at the moment, with the possibility that this may continue at a later date when a long-term plan can be put in place. On the other hand, I am still heavily involved in my other charity Teens Unite Fighting Cancer which I set up with a friend over three years ago. With this we aim to provide respite homes for young adults (thirteen to twenty-four year olds) suffering from life limiting illnesses. They are of an age that is not currently serviced with such facilities, unlike children who have amazing hospices to provide care and respite. We need to focus on what young people want and need. In the meantime, we provide motivational workshops which helps work on their low self-esteem. We also provide trips to things like concerts, sporting events and the theatre, all giving them the opportunity to meet others going through similar dilemmas at this very sensitive time in their lives (www.teensunitefightingcancer.org).

Q. In the book, we cover the topic of how to dress if you are petite in height. As you have in the past spoken about the different clothes that suit your five-foot, two-inch frame, could you offer some more tips to readers on the subject of petite dressing?

A. Yes, being just five foot two inches tall, I do have dressing issues! It's not just about your height, but the build and frame we each have. Some people have equally tiny frames so as long as you are in proportion, you can get away with most things. I'm quite muscular and, for that reason, I find that girly feminine clothes don't really suit me that much and I so opt for a more androgynous look. I have always favoured trousers over skirts, although

I will wear dresses when the occasion calls for it. Trousers give me height particularly when worn with heels. I would normally wear one colour throughout to elongate the look rather than break it up with separate colours. This can be frustrating at times however when I do try to break it up it never feels right, even down to shoe colour. I think darker colours generally help to create the illusion of a long, slim frame. When I want to bring another colour into a look, I might wear a different colour scarf or a different colour handbag. I try to steer away from clothes that have too much colour as the best styles for me tend to be more tailored which is harder at the moment when fashion is moving towards a fuller silhouette. At least these days fashion is far broader than it once was, but I do think it's important to wear what suits rather than what's on trend. We can generically adapt fashion and trends to suit our shapes and sizes.

Q. In the book, we deal with the importance of good posture and the beauty of smiling. Can you tell us how a woman's posture and her smile can affect her overall image?

A. It goes without saying that a happy person with a smile portrays beauty. Posture is key to how we look and feel about ourselves. It shows our confidence and inner feelings about who we are and how we want to be perceived.

Q. What are the main lessons you have learned about fashion and the fashion industry throughout the years you have been involved in your business?

A. I learned that this is a very tough and competitive business, but I guess like any business, to be at the top of your game, you have to work very hard and never become complacent. Fashion can be very diverse and I think it's important that you don't lose sight of your goals. I think it would be easy to diversify into other areas but you need to make sure that you don't spread yourself too thin and dilute the area in which you initially held your strengths. I think one of the main contributing factors of building a successful business in fashion was understanding all aspects of the garment and having an eye for detail, understanding the cut, fabric, construction and also the retail side of things. We have total control through design, manufacture and retail which is, or was, very rare.

Q. What mistakes do women repeatedly make when it comes to fashion?

A. I think as women we need to first take a long good look at ourselves and our bodies. We need to understand our strengths and our weaknesses and figure out how to get the best from them. One mistake that is quite common amongst women is following trends that may not suit them. Perhaps we don't spend enough time researching the styles that are best suited to different sizes, shapes and ages.

We need to experiment more and try new things. Quite quickly it will become obvious what does work and what doesn't. With this

"The best colour in the whole wide world is the one that looks good – on you."

Coco Chanel

FOLLOW THE RULES…

- Steer clear of the colour red if you are prone to blushing or if you have a slightly red complexion. Red always looks best against pale skin tones.

- Dressing in darker colours is often seen as a good way of disguising the parts of our bodies that we find most unflattering. After all, black, navy and grey have traditionally been seen as slimming colours. The reality, however, is that you are not limited to these three colours when it comes to slimming your frame. (In fact all colours are slimming when they are in a slightly darker shade.) The trick is to combine the darker shades with colourful ones. For example, if you like your waist but hate your legs, then wear dark trousers with a bright top. Immediately, the attention is focused on your waist and upper torso.

- When wearing white, pay close attention to your undergarments. There's a long-running myth that you should only wear white underwear beneath a white outfit. Unfortunately, even white underwear will still show through. Instead, it is always best to wear nude-coloured underwear. Try to look for a shade of nude that closely resembles your skin tone.

A brown dress is brought to life with a belt and a bright coat.

- If you are naturally pale skinned, then avoid wearing pastels as these will only leave you looking drawn and washed out. The colours you wear should instead emphasise your natural skin tone. To determine whether or not a particular colour works for you, hold the outfit near your face. Does it look good against your complexion or does it make you look tired and dull?

- If you don't normally wear bright colours in public, then don't throw yourself in the deep end by wearing your new brightly coloured floral dress on a night out. You will only spend the entire time feeling incredibly self-conscious. The day before you plan to debut your dress, wear it around the house first. Make a point of frequently looking in the mirror so that you can accustom your eyes to the new and more colourful you! When the time comes for you to wear the dress on a night out, you should feel far more confident in your brighter shade.

- If you are completely new to wearing colour, take things gradually. Start by wearing a colourful scarf or a piece of jewellery and give yourself time to figure out what colours suit your complexion. Don't forget the key rule I mentioned in the accessories section (page 93): If your necklace or scarf is quite loud then treat it as the statement piece and keep the rest of your outfit plain.

- Even though black is a popular colour in every wardrobe, it doesn't always suit every complexion. As a person matures, wearing black close to the face can sometimes make the complexion appear drained. If this is the case for you, then opt for navy or dark grey.

1. If black is too harsh on your complexion, follow Ellen Barkin's footsteps and wear navy. If you still prefer black, wear it only on your lower half, like Tina Brown.
2. Jennifer Saunders, looking stylish in navy.
3. Nicole Ritchie uses a headscarf to make a colour statement.

115

- If you are wearing one colour from head to toe, then make sure your accessories are of a different shade. Remember, Angelina Jolie at the 2009 Oscar Awards? She wore a beautiful simple black floor length gown with bright emerald green earrings. Without doubt, the earrings made the outfit.

- Unless you are very slim, large prints will only make your frame appear bigger.

- Black is a classic colour and one that is almost fail-safe, but, when it begins to fade, it automatically loses its appeal. Unfortunately, the biggest threat to black fabrics is washing. In order to help preserve the colour of the more costly black items in your wardrobe, have them dry cleaned or spot pressed rather than leaving them at the mercy of your washing machine.

- If you are wearing a dark shade, then a colourful bag is a brilliant way of injecting life into your look, particularly if you're relatively new to wearing bright colours. It is also a useful method of diverting attention away from your figure.

- If you are conscious of your weight, stay away from shiny fabrics as these will add weight to your frame. Matt fabrics are best for disguising weight.

"Fashion has become too sophisticated, too serious. Lighten up! You should enjoy it like a good wine!"

John Galliano

Katherine Jenkins brightens up her white dress with a splash of pink.

116

JEN KELLY, HAUTE COUTURE DESIGNER

In the large beautiful confines of Jen Kelly's eighteenth-century studio, long clothes rails line the walls, each one containing a plethora of stunning pieces. Each and every design looks like it belongs on the iconic frames of past icons such as Audrey Hepburn, Ursula Andress and Marilyn Monroe not to mention the current icons such as Melania Trump, Heidi Klum and Carla Bruni.

His designs, along with his choice of fabrics, are the mark of incredible taste. Whether it's a lace and chiffon wedding gown, a luxury cashmere camel coat or an opulent velvet opera robe, his studio is where timeless fashion is born.

While Jen's creations have certainly sealed his reputation as a world-class haute couture designer, he is first and foremost an enthusiastic symbol of positivity and zest. You cannot but feel so much better after just a few minutes in his company.

Even though Jen grew up in Derry during the height of the Troubles, the political unrest never seemed to interfere with his dreams and goals in life. He is now determined to see that today's young people are also encouraged to overcome their obstacles and follow their dreams.

There's no denying that this designer certainly makes for an outstanding role model. His phenomenal success has come about through hard graft, pure talent and a genius eye for creating the kind of garments that can completely transform a woman. Given that he has created many gowns for Saudi Arabian royalty, it's fair to say that this is one designer who knows exactly how to make a woman look and feel like a princess!

"We must take a step back in order to go forward."

Q. What first inspired your love of fashion? Is it true that you attended the Christian Brothers School with a copy of *Vogue* in your schoolbag?

A. Yes! When I was twelve years old, one of the Christian Brothers found a copy of *Vogue* hidden in amongst my schoolbooks. I remember trying to explain to them that it was just about fashion! I was fortunate in that I had a wonderful teacher called Brother Connolly who always encouraged me in art and design. I was never inhibited. My mother was also a fantastic inspiration because she absolutely loved clothes. My talent was really nurtured and encouraged at a young age, which was hugely important. I now feel very strongly about encouraging talents in children. They are our future and, as such, they should be treasured.

Q. Can you outline the main advantages of investing in haute couture?

A. When you're having something made, you can have whatever you want. That's the joy of it. You don't have to choose from something I have already made, you can come in and share with me your own ideas and we will work together to create something that is tailored specifically for you. I always make the design in calico first so the client always has plenty of opportunities to make changes before it gets to the fabric stage.

Anything you want, you can have. When I am designing, I never see the size of a woman; I just see how I can make her more beautiful. My designs don't translate into a ready-to-wear collection that fits everyone because I like to see the person first and then create a garment to suit them.

Designing is my absolute passion. Regardless of whether it's a wedding dress or a coat, no task is too big or small; my team and I will always go to any lengths to have it just right for the client. It's worth it when a woman tries on your dress and you see their face just light up; that's what it's all about! Couture is made specifically for the individual; it's designed to make you feel special. It's my craft and I'm very proud of it.

Q. You have often spoken of the difference between couture in Ireland and couture in Paris. Personally, I think the quality of Irish couture could easily rival that of New York, Milan and Paris. As a couture designer, what do you find are the main differences?

A. We are an island nation, we have an innate heritage to linens, wools and rustic fibres, whereas if you think of the French or the Italians, it's more smooth.

I think that's the success of Lainey Keogh with her wonderful knits. That's what makes us innately different to European or Mediterranean designers or even American designers. I'm very proud of my Irish heritage. A lot of designers produce their collections abroad but I think it's important to promote a sense of Irishness which is why I produce my clothes in Ireland. There is a lot more to come from Irish designers.

In fact, what I have seen coming from colleges and schools is very encouraging. I think it's very important that when students leave college, the government steps in for approximately two years and give them a platform to exploit their work. The government has subsidised their education and made it inexpensive but yet when they leave, there's nothing for them. The government immediately begins taxing them without giving them the chance to find their feet within the industry. This is stamping out a lot of talent. I think they should be given two years to get themselves set up. Their dreams are being taken away too quickly. I also believe there should be a fashion orientation course available for kids who don't want to go to college; a course that would help them prepare for the industry. Big businesses in Ireland should really be encouraged to go into schools and help these kids through. These students are their future and from a marketing perspective, it's a missed opportunity.

Q. Previously, in an interview, you said something that really stuck with me. You said, "If you don't pursue your dream, you become greatly frustrated. I felt I had to find mine."

A. If you are not true to yourself in doing what you do then you're not going to do it well. For instance, I was once a trainee accountant, but I was so bored by the job that I actually used to fall asleep while doing the books! At the time, however, I thought it was the kind of job that I had to do in order to make a living. I quickly realised that it was not for me!

I'm not precious about my craft or my designs, I do it because I love it. It makes people happy. I hate it when designers are tied to nothing other than making money. There should be a legacy to what you do, and the greats, such as Valentino and Sybil Connolly, are perfect examples of this.

Body and Beauty

Skincare

ASK THE EXPERT...
DR ROSEMARY COLEMAN,
LEADING SKINCARE SPECIALIST

Dr Rosemary Coleman is based in the Blackrock Clinic in Dublin.

"Nature gives you the face you have at twenty; it is up to you to merit the face you have at fifty."

Coco Chanel

Q. What tips would you offer to women in their teens and twenties who want to have good skin in years to come?

A. Sun block, sun block and more sun block. I consider SPF the best anti-ageing cream. In fact, if you did nothing else but use rigorous sun block for a year, you would notice a change in your skin. Wrinkles would begin to reverse. You should also wear sun block on your neck and hands. When you're driving, your hands are directly exposed to UV rays through the windscreen because they're on the steering wheel. You need to reapply because when you go to the bathroom, you will wash it off. If you don't take care of them, your hands and neck will reveal your true age.

Secondly, take off your make-up before you go to bed, making sure that you have removed it carefully. Don't pull or drag the skin especially around the eye area. When it

Top Tip

You should always wear sun block on your neck and hands. When you are driving, the position of your hands on the steering wheel leaves them directly exposed to UV rays through the windscreen. It's also very important to reapply sun block to your hands throughout the day. If you don't take care of them, your hands and neck will reveal your true age in years to come.

comes to teenagers, remember they are still growing so it's best to keep their routine simple otherwise you will strip the skin. Teenagers today wear a lot of make-up but there's a good chance that it is providing them with photo protection. Unfortunately, however, we haven't seen enough generations of it to know whether or not they are all going to end up with clogged pores. You also have to remember that most of the products are far better than they were years ago, so if your teenager is using decent products that are appropriate for their skin type, then they should not be clogging their pores or causing acne cosmetica (creating acne by using the wrong products).

My opinion is that you can age very elegantly if you have a good complexion. Cut down on alcohol as this dehydrates the skin. Smoking likewise is as bad for your skin as the sun. I always encourage patients to increase their intake of water. It's so important for both healthy skin and mind. In fact, there's a great saying: "The solution to pollution is dilution." It basically means that drinking a lot water will flush out the toxins and keep your mind alert. A good tip is to have a glass of water for every cup of tea or coffee you drink.

Overall, I cannot emphasise enough just how important it is to wear sun block every day, even on those cloudy days where UVA is still coming straight through the clouds. If you go for a long walk without wearing sun block or make-up, you will have freckles and pigmentation by the end of it. I would never dream of leaving the house without sun block. My advice to everyone is to wear it regardless

of the weather. Rather than using a separate moisturiser and sun block, simplify your morning regime and use a moisturiser with high SPF protection. Don't forget to reapply it throughout the day as well, particularly if you are spending a lot of time outside. It's a good idea to buy a spray-on SPF. This is much easier to apply regularly throughout the day.

Q. Are cleansing and toning important?

A. No. Toning is really only important if you have oily skin. A lot of toners also have alcohol in them and I certainly wouldn't put that near my skin. Toners are really only beneficial for people with prominent pores or a greasy complexion.

Q. Can you talk to us about adult acne? What are the main aggravators of it and what are the various treatments available to help eradicate it? You mentioned in the past that some women notice their acne disappearing when they cut out lattes from their diet!

A. Quite a lot of teenagers get acne but that doesn't mean that they should have it. After all, it is a condition that damages the skin. If your child was left with a scar following a fire, you would walk the length and breadth of the country to find someone who could get rid of it, so why on earth would you sit back and watch your son or daughter suffer from acne which is a condition that basically eats away holes in their skin? People think it doesn't bother boys as much as girls, but it does. It damages their self-esteem enormously. I have plenty of men asking me to treat their acne scars.

You can actually have acne scarring as a teenager and not realise how bad it is until you get older. As you age, you start to lose collagen and elastic tissue and, as a result, your skin decompensates and loses volume. Consequently, it unmasks the scars that were not so obvious when your face was slightly plumper. The reality is that the daily diet of younger people is not as healthy as it was twenty years ago and more. I know when I was a child, we certainly didn't have the same level of sugar in our diets that kids today have. The main foods categories that I associate with acne would be sugar, dairy and nuts.

A common area for acne is the chin. Women will often find that prior to their period they will get spots on either side of their chin. Why? Well again, diet plays a part. I call it 'acne latte' because lattes are full of milk and hormones and a lot of my patients notice that their acne disappears after they give them up. I don't allow my children to drink milk because it's full of sugar and fat. We are the only mammals to continue drinking milk after we have been weaned. Nuts are another big contributor to acne, particularly peanuts and peanut butter. Overall, your skin will reflect what you eat. You cannot eat junk all day and expect your skin to look healthy.

Q. What is the best treatment for acne?

A. The best treatment for acne is medication. It's the most effective and the cheapest. There are other elements than can be brought into the treatment process such as skincare and diet, as well as ancillary treatments such as micro-dermabrasion and photodynamic therapy. When I have a patient who isn't responding to medication, or who cannot take medication, I can offer them other treatments but they are usually more expensive, more time consuming and less effective.

Q. Parents are often worried about the drugs being prescribed to their teenagers for skin conditions, such as acne. What advice could you offer them?

A. Trust your doctor and take the medication s/he recommends. They have your child's best interest at heart and they're not going to give them medication that is dangerous for them. Just don't sit back and let your child suffer with acne. There has been a lot of hype recently about Roaccutane, which is prescribed for treating acne, but it's only hype. I have taken it in the past and I would have no problem giving it to my kids.

Q. In relation to cosmetic surgery, is there one part of the face that women are always trying to improve?

A. The frown is the one area most people want treated. This is the most common request by a long way. Botox is quite good for both the frown and the Marionette lines near the mouth. Marionette actually means 'sad clown' and it's with good reason that those lines are called that! They alone can make you look sad and grumpy. Crows feet are not the worst lines to have. If anything, they can make a person's eyes more twinkly. Sometimes, I think a person looks better with them!

Botox takes about two minutes and can be carried out during your lunch break. You could go straight into a meeting and no one would know you had it done. You would have three puffy dots for a few minutes but that's the extent of the after-effects.

Q. When it comes to cosmetic procedures, it goes without saying that the procedure has to be tailored to suit the person, but how do you go about doing that? What aspects do you take into consideration?

A. First of all, I would never recommend making drastic changes to the face. What I think we should be doing is trying to get back a little of what we have lost rather than striving for what we never had in the first place. If a woman with very thin lips handed me a photograph of Angelina Jolie or Scarlett Johansson and said, "I want those lips", I wouldn't do it for her. The maximum age for your lips is fourteen, after that your lips are on the way down. If I have a patient in their forties who has nice full lips, I usually ask them if they were hounded at school about it. They will almost always tell me they were teased endlessly and called names like 'rubber lips'. As they got older, however, they began to see their lips as a more beautiful feature. But, if you never had those kind of lips, then it's like trying to inflate a small balloon. It will look distorted and unbalanced on the face. If, on the other hand, you are just trying to restore what was once there, then it's much safer.

I think it's better to tweak your look rather than change it. My attitude is that you should do as little as you have to in order to create the look you want. The moment you start doing more than you need to, you're in trouble.

Q. Sometimes women in their forties and fifties might think it's too late to start improving their skin. Does age matter or can anyone improve the appearance of their skin?

A. My oldest cosmetic patient is ninety-two years old. She is using the Sculptra treatment. This is a new procedure that has been nicknamed 'the liquid facelift'. It's fantastic in that it basically restores the volume and the softness to the face. Men in their sixties also come in to me for treatment. It's never too late to start!

Q. How often should you get a mole checked?

A. It's very simple. Visit your doctor, the second you notice a change.

Q. There are so many brands available in terms of skincare. How can we determine the best types to go for?

A. Rely on the good brands like Roc, La Roche Posay, Hamilton, Soltan SPF. La Roche Posay for instance is a very high-quality, low-price brand. Word of mouth is also a good way of discovering good products, however it really comes down to finding out what suits you. For example, I was given a very well-known brand with an SPF factor of fifty-seven, and yet I burned through it. It's a good product but it just didn't suit my skin.

Q. What are the main skin conditions you see being presented to you in your clinic?

A. I see every condition – hair, skin and nails – at my clinic but the most common ones are roseacia, red faces and acne.

Marilyn Monroe

Beauty

I've always said it – if you want to take years off your appearance, get yourself the right make-up colours and learn the tricks on how to apply them. Before I armed myself with the right application skills, I would just dip the brush in some eye shadow and apply it directly to the eyelid without giving thought to blending and shading. These days, however, I know exactly how to alter my colours and achieve the looks I want. Believe me, something as simple as using eyeliner or even just wearing the right shade of foundation can really make a huge difference to your face.

ASK THE EXPERT... PAULA CALLAN O'KEEFFE, MAKE-UP ARTIST & CO-OWNER OF BROWN SUGAR SALON

Q. How should a woman prepare her face before applying make-up?

A. There are so many primers on the market at the moment but, for me, the best primer is moisturiser. In my opinion, there's no need to apply loads of lotions before putting on your foundation. The most important thing is to ensure your skin is in its best condition. Think of your skin as a canvas and your make-up as the paint. If the canvas is rough and in bad condition, it won't suddenly look good when you apply paint over it.

You need to exfoliate your skin once a week and always use a good moisturiser. If your skin is very oily or dry, there are plenty of specific treatments you can avail of to help your complexion look its best. Just make sure you always use SPF and a really good moisturiser. I personally find that the cheaper moisturisers give the best results.

Q. How can a woman prevent that 'caked on' look when applying her make-up?

A. One of my pet hates is seeing a woman wear a shade of foundation that doesn't suit her skin tone. It looks so horrendous that I think wearing no foundation is actually much better than wearing the wrong one. Ironically, some women aren't even aware that they are using far too much. If you use a foundation in

the way in which it is supposed to be used, then it should look like it isn't even there. A foundation is supposed to enhance your natural features, not cover them up. If you're left with a make-up line along the jaw bone, take it as a sign that you have too much on.

To be honest, I think concealer is more important than foundation. A lot of women prefer to apply their concealer underneath their foundation, however I prefer to apply it after because I find the foundation provides a nice base for the concealer to touch up. Next, I always use powder. For everyday wear, you need to finish the look with powder because it sets the foundation and completes the look.

I often find that a lot of women rush a part of their make-up to get to the part they like. For example, some women like doing their eyes, so they will rush the foundation part, or they might rush the eyes to get to the lips. I think it pays to take your time with each and every single element of the makeup process.

Q. Should foundation be applied with a brush or a sponge?

A. I always say 'each to their own', but my preference is to use a brush.

Q. How can our readers achieve make-up artist results at home?

A. When it comes to make-up, I think every woman should invest in good brushes. Imagine a highly skilled carpenter using cheap tools – he might have the ability, but if his tools are not up to standard, the results won't be good. The same goes for make-up. I cannot understand women who use secondary tools to apply expensive cosmetics to their face. They just won't achieve good results.

Good brushes will last you a lifetime if cared for properly. I still use the brushes that I bought on my first day working for MAC some years ago and they still work just as well now as they did back then. Ideally, you should wash your brushes once a week. The best way to clean the bristles is to buy a brush cleanser, however this can be a bit pricey so a great inexpensive way of cleaning them is to use a dollop of shampoo and some warm water. Make sure you rinse them really well, otherwise you risk leaving a residue on the brush hair. If you use a make-up sponge for your foundation, always wash

the sponge every few days. Any brush that is being constantly dipped into liquid, needs to be washed frequently. Eye-shadow brushes on the other hand don't need to be washed as often because they're only being dipped into powder.

Q. What is the lifespan of mascara when it has been opened?

A. The rule is six to eight weeks. A lot of mascaras will begin to dry out after that amount of time. After eight weeks, bugs and germs start to develop in the mascara tube which can be dangerous when applied to the eyes. In fact, if you looked at these bugs under a microscope, you would never want them near your eyes again. Don't ever allow anyone to use your mascara. Conjunctivitis, for example, is so contagious. In our Brown Sugar salon, we always use disposable mascara wands.

Q. What is the best way to apply blusher?

A. Blusher should be applied to the apples of the cheeks and then blended in with a powder brush. When choosing the right shade for your skin, always remember that blusher should look like your own natural blush. Using blusher to contour, shade and highlight can give your face a really good shape but that's a whole other area of skill.

A simple way to contour your face is to imagine a line that starts at the top of your ear and goes down to the corner of your mouth. That's the line you apply your blusher to when you want to give some definition to your cheekbones. When it comes to make-up, it's really all about angles.

Q. What advice would you offer to women who are afraid to experiment with different make-up styles and colours?

A. There are women who change their clothes every season but yet have been wearing the same make-up for twenty years. I really believe women should have their make-up applied by a professional twice a year. That way they can see what colours suit them. It also gives them the chance to ask for advice about what colours are in season and to see how the different products are applied. Women have often said to me, after I had applied their make-up, "I never thought of applying it like that."

I work with colour all the time, so I know instantly what colours will suit a person. Sometimes, women need someone else to point it out to them because they don't realise it themselves.

It's not uncommon for women to bring in a picture of a celebrity and ask for the same make-up style. Regardless of the make-up style, I think everything can be adapted, but I don't think you should repeat a look exactly as before. It's much better to adapt it to suit the face. I could do the same make-up style on ten women, but it would look totally different on each woman because I would have adapted it to suit their faces and individuality. Women should bear this in mind whenever they are trying to replicate a celebrity make-up look.

Q. What advice would you offer to a woman who wants to change her make-up look?

A. You have to remember your skin is always changing. What looked good on you when you were twenty won't look as good on you when you're thirty or forty. In fact, it will age you. However, if you update your make-up, you will look so much younger than you would if you went out and got a facelift. If I spoke to someone who was thinking about getting a facelift, I would immediately advise them to

Paula applying diamonds to a model...

...getting ready for the photoshoot...

.. the finished result.

instead get their make-up done professionally, get a good eyebrow shaping and then a really good, updated haircut. A good make-up style can take years off you. If you have it done professionally, always ask them what products they are using so that you can recreate it at home. It's always a good idea to ask the make-up artist if they provide lessons in applying make-up. Most make-up artists will offer lessons for a reasonable price.

Q. How can a woman create a beautiful classic look?

A. Use colours that are tones of your own skin colour. It's like when you see a celebrity pictured at an awards ceremony and even though you know they are wearing make-up, it actually looks like they're not wearing any. This is because their make-up artist found the tones to suit their skin. Your make-up should leave you looking like yourself, but just a super-perfect version of your natural self. It's a flawless, natural look. Don't rely on your foundation for colour, use it to emphasise your own skin tones. If you're unsure about the tones, you should be going for, consult with a make-up artist. They should be able to help you determine your individual needs in terms of foundation.

Q. What is the most common make-up mistake made by women?

A. I hate an unfinished look. For example, when a woman has lined her eyes but has not put on mascara. I love make-up to be perfect and complete. I also hate it when people neglect their eyebrows. Your eyebrows are so important because they frame your face. Beautifully groomed eyebrows can make such

a difference, whereas a bad eyebrow shape can ruin your whole look. Bad eyebrows will draw the attention away from your good points.

Q. Can women of all ages use shimmer?

A. You will often hear myths like, "You should never wear shiny eye shadow once you're over thirty." That's rubbish. It's all about how and where you apply the shimmer. I would have absolutely no problem applying shimmer eye shadow on someone over a certain age but I wouldn't apply it from their eyelid to their eyebrow because it would look ridiculous on them and it would also age them. Instead, I would apply a dot of shimmer on the eyelids or maybe a touch of it on the cheekbones. Afterwards, the person will look so fresh because it will have enhanced their overall appearance. The one piece of advice I would offer in relation to shimmer is never to apply it over wrinkles or fine lines as it will only emphasise them.

Q. What make-up tips would you offer to a woman with small eyes?

A. That's a master-class in itself! Some people will tell you that you can't wear smoky eye shadow if your eyes are small, but this just isn't true. If anything, it can make them look bigger. Smoky eyes work beautifully for everyone. Contrary to popular belief, however, the term 'smoky' doesn't just mean black, brown and grey. You can create the smoky look with any colour – purples, pinks, blues or a combination of colours. Everyone should also have an eyelash curler. I couldn't live without mine. It opens up your eyes so much.

LISA'S TIPS... FOR COSMETICS

Perfume

- If, like me, you hate having to reapply perfume time and time again, you will definitely appreciate this little tip. Dab some Vaseline on the areas where you would normally spray your perfume, such as your wrists and neck. When you have done this, apply your perfume as usual. The Vaseline will retain the scent and make it last so much longer!

Perfect primers

- If you suffer from dry patches of skin, use a hydrating primer on the areas in question. If you have an oily T-zone or suffer from oily patches of skin, use a mattifying primer.

Foundation

- If you find that your foundation is rather heavy, use it sparingly by mixing it with your moisturiser.

- When using a tinted moisturiser, don't forget to apply some to your ears. This will give you the appearance of an overall natural colour.

- To assess the coverage potential of different foundations, tilt the bottle and see how it flows. If the liquid flows quite fast and is rather thin in texture, chances are it will only provide you with very light coverage.

- When testing foundations, do not use the back of your hand. The colour of the skin on your hand does not resemble the colour of your complexion and so will not be accurate. Instead, dab some on your lower cheek near your jawbone. This will also give you an indication as to how easily it will blend into the edges of your face.

- Never go for a darker shade of foundation in the hope that it will give you tanned-looking skin. Foundation is quite thick in texture and will be incredibly difficult to blend into the edges of the face if the shade is distinctly darker than your natural skin tone.

- After you have applied your foundation, use a ply of tissue to gently pat your face. This will help soften the look. Also try to apply minimal foundation around the eyes particularly if you have fine lines. The foundation will sink into the lines thereby making them more obvious.

Brushes

- There's nothing more annoying than buying a new make-up brush only to find it shedding bristles the moment it's put to use. Next time you are shopping for a brush and you want to determine if it is prone to shedding, quickly run the bristles along the back of your hand. Try to look for brushes with tightly packed bristles as they are less likely to come apart.

- When washing your brushes, there's a risk they may loose their shape. If this occurs, wrap the bristles tightly in a handkerchief while they are still wet and secure them with an elastic band. This should help to renew the original shape of the brush – but ensure the band is not too tight, otherwise the bristles may loosen.

- Eyeliner brushes may be small but they're still expensive! A wonderful tip given to me by a make-up artist is to look in art and craft shops for slim paint brushes that work perfectly for applying eyeliner.

Concealer

- If you tan regularly, make sure you have a concealer in a shade appropriate for darker skin. If you use your regular concealer on tanned skin, it may result in drawing focus to the blemishes rather than disguising them.

Powder

- When dusting powder on the face, begin at the nose and work your way outwards. By doing this, you are ensuring that the shiniest parts of your face get the most powder.

Lips

- To keep lipstick off your teeth, place your index finger in your mouth and close your lips around it. When you pull your finger out, it will remove any excess lipstick.

- If you're not one for wearing bright lip colours, it's advisable to try red lipstick at home first. Chances are you'll hate it, but only because you're not used to seeing your face wearing such a vivacious colour. For an accurate assessment, leave the lipstick on for an hour. Look in the mirror every so often during that hour and you'll gradually train your eye to it. When the hour is up, you'll be able to tell whether or not a shade suits you.

- When using lip liner, don't limit the colour to the rim of your lips. Fill them in with the liner, then if your lipstick fades, your lips will still have the colour from the liner.

- If you suffer from dry, chapped lips, avoid frosted lipsticks as they tend to dry out the lips.

- If you don't have the lip colour you require, then open up your eye shadow palette and improvise! An age-old trick used by many a make-up artist involves dabbing the lips with Vaseline before lightly blending in the eye shadow colour of choice.

- If you find that your lipstick is a shade darker than you expected, don't throw it away! Apply the lipstick to your lips as usual. Next blend a little foundation with some Vaseline and, using your fingertip, apply it to your lips. This will immediately lighten the shade.

- In order for your lip colour to look its best, your lips need to be in tip-top condition. To soothe and soften dry lips, mix some sugar with Vaseline and gently massage the mix onto your lips. To get the most benefits from this exfoliating paste, apply it to a dry toothbrush first and use it as an exfoliator.

- If you prefer the minimalist approach and like to carry as few products as possible, look out for multi-use items. For instance, buy lip colours with a built-in gloss or balm, or use a tinted moisturiser rather than moisturiser and foundation.

Blush

- To avoid creating a distinctive line when applying blush, work the brush in circular motions on the apples of your cheeks.

Eyebrows

- To give your plucked brows a nice, defined shape brush them upwards and then sideways. You can buy brow brushes, but quite a lot of make-up artists like to use toothbrushes as the bristles are so thick and excellent for shaping.

- To give your brows a glossy shine, apply some Vaseline to a brow brush before sweeping it over your brows. If you find that your brows tend to lose their shape quite fast, spray your brush with hairspray before running it over the brows. The hairspray will secure their shape.

Eyes

- Before applying eye shadow, always prepare the skin on the eyelid by dabbing it with some concealer and lightly dusting it with loose translucent powder.

- If you find that your eye shadow is too dark dab a cotton wool ball in some loose powder and gently blend it into the lid until the colour has toned down.

- If you have mature skin or puffy eyes, avoid frosted shimmery shades of eye shadow, use soft matt shades instead.

- Certain shades of eye shadow can really emphasise your natural eye colour. To help you on your way here is a list of shades that best enhance different eye colours.

Green eyes
Golden brown, mauve, lilac, taupe, violet, deep purple, plum, peach and gold.

Grey eyes
Purple, violet, charcoal, brown, black, pink, blue, gold and light green.

Brown eyes
Brown-eyed girls can wear a variety of eye colours, though violets look particularly well, they can also work the smoky-eye look.

Blue eyes
Chocolate brown, warm taupe, gold, plum, champagne and rich peach. Shimmery gold is perfect for evening occasions. While blue-eyed girls can wear navy eye shadow, they should steer clear of blue shades similar to their own eye colour.

- Good-quality beige and browns should be a staple feature of every woman's make-up palette. These shades are perfect for when you want to add instant definition to your eyes but don't have much time to spend on your eye make-up.

- When applying eye shadow, make sure the brush reaches the roots of the eyelashes otherwise there will be a space between the lashes and the eye shadow which makes the overall impact less intense.

Mascara

- Some women have a preference for the type of mascara wand they use. Some like combs, others like wands. If you want to buy a new mascara but don't like the wand that comes with it, then recycle an old mascara wand you do like. Clean it thoroughly with make-up remover and it's ready to be reused. Just make sure you don't discard the new wand as you will need it to close the mascara.

- If you stain the skin around the eye when applying mascara, wait until it dries before gently wiping it away with cotton wool swab. It will be so much easier to remove when dry. The opposite applies to eyeliner. If you make a mistake with liquid eyeliner, use a swab to remove it immediately, before it dries.

Tanning

ASK THE EXPERT... RACHEL KAVANAGH, CREATOR OF THE ROCKSTAR TAN

- The optimum time to apply fake tan is when your body's Ph level is 4.5 per cent. Most women will have a shower before applying their tan but if they use soap products, this will increase their pH levels to 7 per cent. Remember, your skin needs a pH of 4.5 per cent for the product to work properly, so if you apply tan to skin that has a pH of 7 per cent, you will end up with a nasty orange tan. It will also fade extremely quickly because it won't seep into the skin, it will just sit on the top layer. There are pH balancing sprays on the market that help your skin reach the optimum pH level for tanning when you come out of the shower. If, however, you don't have a pH balancing spray before you tan, then take a damp cloth and run it all over your body or spritz your skin with water. This will hydrate your skin and will help it soak up the tan when it's applied.

- Start building up a fake tan kit in the same way you would build a make-up kit. Acquire all the necessities, such as barrier cream, tanning mitt, tan remover and exfoliating gloves. If you wear tan all the time, then arm yourself with the products that will make it look its best.

- Moisturising is important, however if you want the perfect fake tan, you need to hydrate your skin properly by drinking lots of water. You can have the most moisturised skin in the world but it will be of no benefit if your skin is not properly hydrated as the tan will not seep in. If you start drinking a lot of water, you will notice a massive difference in how the tan appears on your skin.

- When the tan has developed, you need to moisturise every day to keep it looking its best. However, if you have dehydrated skin to begin with, then no amount of moisturiser will save it. You can lather on the moisturiser, but if your skin is already too dry then you are going to have a tough time getting your tan to fade evenly. How it develops and fades will be primarily decided by the preparation and application process.

- Do not use your hands or rubber gloves when applying tan. Get yourself a tanning mitt. They can be bought in any chemist and you will notice a difference in the results. When you spray the tan onto you skin, do not rub it in. Pat it and blend. The less heat friction you create, the better.

- A tanning spray, by its very nature, will always be darker than a tanning mousse. If you're pale skinned, a mousse tan will give you a nice glow. If, however, you want a darker tan, then buy a tan in the form of a spray bottle. One layer of tan from a spray bottle should suffice. You may need two layers of mousse, particularly around the chest area.

- We all strive for a beautiful colour. After all, a good fake tan can make you look slimmer and healthier. What people need to realise, however, is that going heavy on the fake tan will not make it last longer. It will actually make it fade faster and nastier. There is no point layering on the fake tan because it's the DHA ingredient in the tan that will turn you brown and this does not fully develop until after about fourteen hours. Your skin can only take a certain amount. Tan not only sits on the top layer of the skin, it goes 25 per cent into the skin; that's why it lasts a few days. There is the cosmetic bronzer which is the colour guide you immediately see when you apply it to the skin. However, that will wash away when you step into the shower.

- People with snow white skin have to learn to accept that they will never have sallow skin. Stop trying to be golden brown if you are naturally pale. Wear the amount that suits you. If you don't wear so much of it, you can easily wear tan every day.

- If you have very sensitive skin then you need to look out for fake tans that are non-comedogenic because otherwise the cosmetic bronzer in the tan may clog your pores or leave you with an allergic reaction.

- Never apply moisturiser directly before applying your fake tan, otherwise the colour will slide off. Moisturise the night before, but not on the same day.

- It's often the case that fake tan will gather in certain parts of the body such as hands, wrists, elbows and knees. To prevent these dark patches from occurring, use a fake tan barrier cream. Apply it to the most troublesome areas and it will prevent your skin from absorbing too much tan. It will give you an even tan overall which can be very difficult to achieve otherwise. If you don't have barrier cream, then apply moisturiser to a cotton pad and dab it on your hands, feet and elbows. It will help you achieve a realistic looking tan.

- If you want to apply fake tan to your face, then only do so very lightly. If you apply foundation and powder over heavy tan, it will end up looking quite grey. You will also end up with a caked look. This is why make-up artists always tell brides not to have fake tan on their face.

- DHA is such a volatile ingredient in fake tan. For instance, if you leave the top off the tanning bottle and too much air gets in, you could be left with a green tint when you apply it to your skin.

- Any product with oil or chlorine will strip fake tan very fast. Oils will seep into the skin and lift the tan so make sure your moisturisers or lotions do not contain oils if you are using them on skin that has been fake tanned.

- Sometimes women think a fake tan doubles up as protection from the sun. It doesn't. You still need your SPF. Just make sure your tan has fully developed before you apply any moisturisers and lotions.

DIY exfoliators

Exfoliating is absolutely vital when it comes to achieving healthy-looking skin and is also a necessary part of pre-tan preparation. I always love how soft and refreshed my skin feels after I have exfoliated away the dry, dead skin. In fact, using a dry-brush exfoliator is a fantastic way of invigorating the circulation and giving you that boost of energy after a long day. If, however, you are very conscious of the chemicals that are used in skincare products, then why not go organic and make your own exfoliators?

The exact amount for each ingredient depends on how much you want to use. Remember, it's meant to be a scrub so the texture should be quite thick.

- Honey is wonderful for the skin which is why it's a must for any body scrub. Combine it with sugar and you will have healthy looking skin in no time. If you want to go a step further, add in some olive oil and coconut essence. It will smell beautiful when combined with the honey.

- Mix some sugar with your favourite shower lotion. If you want your skin to feel extremely soft and silky, substitute the shower lotion for olive oil.

- Sea sand and olive oil. Add in some almond essence for a beautiful scent that lingers on your skin.

- Oatmeal and water is a brilliant facial scrub but also doubles up as a soft body scrub. For a wonderfully refreshing pick me up, add in some lemon juice or peppermint essence.

- For incredibly silky skin, mix together some sugar and baby oil. The sugar will do the exfoliating work while the baby oil will leave your skin moisturised and smooth.

- If you're looking for luxury in a scrub, then you will love this particular mixture. Mash three strawberries and add in eight spoons of sugar. Fold in approximately five teaspoons of almond essence (or, if you prefer, vanilla essence). When complete, massage the mixture into the skin for about five to ten minutes before rinsing.

Hair

I'm not the biggest fan of my hair. In fact, most mornings, it refuses downright to co-operate with me.

Thanks to years of products and processing, it's quite dry and brittle but, fortunately I'm blessed with friends who are talented hairstylists! Two of these friends are Mark O'Keeffe, from Brown Sugar, and Gary Kavanagh, Creative Director at Peter Mark. I don't know how, but they manage to whip my tresses into shape any time I'm heading to an event and need it looking its best. Given the miracles they perform on my hair, I couldn't think of two people more qualified to offer advice on hair styling!

Q. What is the one mistake women make time and time again?

Gary Kavanagh (GK) The one point I always make to customers is that regardless of what product you are using, always read the label. If it says 'leave on for eight minutes', people will usually sit down and watch television for half an hour thinking that the longer they leave it in, the better the results. The reality, however, is that the product stops working and will then have the opposite effect on your hair. The label says eight minutes because this is when the product is at its best. Remember, companies spend thousands upon thousands researching and establishing the exact time required for the product to work its best. If you were cooking and the recipe stipulated a cooking time of thirty minutes, you wouldn't leave the dish in the oven for an hour thinking you would get better results! Stick to be instructions. This is particularly important in relation to hair colour. If you are applying a home hair colour and it says leave on for twenty minutes, it most certainly does not mean leave on for half an hour.

Mark O'Keeffe

Gary Kavanagh

"Hairstyle is the final tip-off whether or not a woman really knows herself."

Hubert de Givenchy

Q. What are your tips for achieving and maintaining volume in hair?

GK If you don't have natural volume in your hair, it is imperative that you rinse your conditioner thoroughly, otherwise you will quickly lose whatever volume you later achieve through styling. Also make sure that you are using the correct conditioner. Your hair might need a light conditioner rather than a strong one, or it might even only need a conditioning spray so be sure to buy the one that's right for you. There are a lot of products out there that are conditioning body builders. Miracle Mist by GHD and Prep by Bumble & Bumble are two really good body-building conditioners.

It's also important to remember that your scalp will become quite warm because a lot of body heat escapes through the top of your head. If there is residual conditioner in your hair, the heat will make it greasy, thereby destroying the volume.

You can also combine your products. After you use some Miracle Mist, follow it up with a blow-drying lotion. Comb the lotion through the hair and then blow dry the roots first. The big secret is to dry the roots first! Lift the hair with a round brush and get the heat right into the roots.

Bumble & Bumble also have a Prep and Tonic which is really good for the scalp. If you have a clean, healthy scalp then you will have clean, healthy hair.

Mark O'Keeffe (M O'K) There are loads of volumising products on the market. To get good results, you usually just comb the product into the roots and let it sit before washing it out. Then there are products that you spritz into the roots before blasting the hair with a blow-dryer. There are also many different ways to blow dry volume into your hair. Some women prefer to use tongs or heated rollers to inject the hair with loads of body. It comes down to skill factor and how good you are with styling your hair. I think rollers are particularly good for volume and very easy to use. Heated rollers are the best and they are so inexpensive, but if you don't have them, you can use a blow-dryer on your hair when the rollers are in. It's far more convenient, however, to use the pre-heated rollers because during the fifteen minutes they are in your hair, you can use the time to paint your nails or do your make-up rather than wasting time holding a blow-dryer on the ordinary rollers.

A lot of women backcomb their hair to try and give it body but that's one of the ways to cause hair damage. Backcombing is a skill in itself and there is a correct way to do it without damaging the hair. Women usually just put the comb in and start vigorously pushing the hair up and down. That just creates a bird-nest type mound of hair and that's not how backcombing is done. Backcombing is done by putting the comb in the hair, pushing it down, taking the comb out again, and pushing the next layer down on top of it. You are basically stacking the hair. When backcombing is done right, it's so easy to brush it out when you're finished with the look, but when backcombing is done incorrectly, it just creates knots and tangles.

There are some great dry shampoos on the market which are brilliant for giving your hair volume as well as one or two extra days of life.

Q. Does rinsing your hair with cold water really make a difference?

M O'K Yes. The cold water will close the cuticle layer of the hair and, as a result, will reflect light and shine. Rinsing your hair with cold water is also very good for your scalp because it closes the scalp pores.

Brown Sugar

Q. What is the best way to keep hair looking its very best?

GK To keep hair in optimum condition, I would always recommend that people use a clearing shampoo once a week to get rid of all the gunge in the hair. Sometimes, people use a clearing shampoo every day, thinking their hair will benefit even more but what they're doing is wrong. Their hair will only end up feeling really dry. There's a great clearing spray by Bumble & Bumble called Sunday because you're only supposed to use it once a week, i.e. Sunday. Celebrities make a point of taking care of their hair and this is precisely why their tresses always look so great.

Q. Can you talk to us about the twelve-week blow-dry? Is it all hype or does it work?

M O'K It has been around for such a long time and was known as the Brazilian Treatment but then some marketing genius called it the twelve-week blow-dry and that's when it really took off. To be honest, I think it should be called 'the world's best conditioning treatment ever'! It's made of natural ingredients except the preserve which stops it from going off before the twelve weeks are up. On the right client, it can work wonders. It is brilliant for getting rid of frizz and making your hair very silky and smooth. However, it does depend on the client and what results they are looking for. If they want a big blow-dry then it's not going to last as long. If the client has fine hair or oily limp hair, then the treatment will only cause their hair stick to their scalp. This is why a consultation is so important because you need to find out what kind of results the client is looking for. If the client wants dead straight hair that looks really healthy then this is the treatment for them.

GK All the results I have seen it produce so far have been very good. It shouldn't be called the twelve-week blow-dry because it gives the impression that your blow-dry will last twelve weeks. Of course your blow dry won't last that long. What it will do, however, is make your hair much more manageable for twelve weeks because it softens down the hair leaving it looking in great condition. Just make sure that your hairstylist is experienced and knows exactly what they are doing. The treatment takes about two hours to complete and the stylist has to be meticulous about the way in which they apply the lotion. It is a bit of fad and I'm sure in six months time, there will be some new craze. There's no doubt about it though, this treatment definitely works.

Q. What hair styling tools and products should every woman own?

M O'K This depends on how good a person is at styling their hair and what they want to do with their hair. If they want straight hair, then they should invest in a paddle brush or good straightening irons as these will make life very easy for them. Heat protection is vital when you are using such heat on your hair. L'Oréal Techni Hot Style Constructor spray is absolutely brilliant for protecting hair against heat damage. When using hair straighteners, always use them in the same way you would use a hot iron on a delicate silk blouse. Run the straighteners through the hair in one gentle swift movement. Don't ever drag them

through the hair slowly. This is a mistake women often make.

Q. Are hairbrushes with boars' bristles, natural bristles, synthetic bristles... but is there a noticeable difference in terms of results? What is the best kind of bristle to have in a hairbrush?

GK In general, bristles do not break hair, people do. I usually try to steer people away from brushes with plastic bristles as they tend to cause static, especially on hair that is quite dry. Boars' hair bristles are by far the best. When you are buying a hairbrush, it's important to feel the bristles. Good bristles should feel quite soft. You don't necessarily have to go to a hairdressing supplies shop to get good hairbrushes, although admittedly you would be better off doing so because they will have a far bigger range. Whenever you're buying a hairbrush, just read the label and it will tell you if it is 100 per cent bristle or 75 per cent bristle. If you take care of your brushes, they will last for ever!

Q. Is it damaging to wash your hair every day?

M O'K No, that's an old wives tale. Years and years ago, shampooing every day would have been very damaging for hair because, back then, products were harsh. In fact, back then, a lot of women would have washed their hair with detergent or soap because nice shampoos were not available. So in those days, yes it would have been very damaging to wash it every day, but, today, there's nothing wrong with doing so because the products are made specifically for hair and are not in any want to keep the years off your appearance, then move with the times. This goes for make-up and clothes as well as hairstyles.

Q. A lot of women are using hair extensions. What's the best way to care for the extensions? Can women continue using their usual shampoo or do they need special products?

M O'K There are special products on the market for extensions but most extensions are made from natural hair so it's perfectly fine to use your usual shampoo and conditioner. The downside to hair extensions is that they can damage your hair. To secure the hair in place, the stylist applies an artificial glue. Generally when hair extensions come out, you are left with a lot of broken hair because pulling and tugging the hair will eventually cause it to snap. This has nothing to do with how the extensions were applied in the first place, it's all to do with general wear and tear, which is very hard to avoid.

Mark O'Keeffe and Brown Sugar staff at the L'Oréal Professionnel Colour Trophy finals.

Q. What advice would you offer to someone who is considering a drastic change of hairstyle?

GK Never make a dramatic change to your hair on impulse. If you want to make a dramatic change to your hair colour, talk it through with your hairdresser first. Maybe start off with a few low lights and then continue gradually from there before going the whole way. In a few months time you might completely change your mind and decide you don't like the colour at all. It's also a good idea to review what you want to have. A lot of people aim too high outside their boundaries of possibility. Work out your options and establish the ideal style for your face. Aim for the achievable. Don't go for a Jennifer Aniston hairstyle if your face is mostly suited to a bob haircut. Be realistic with yourself. Remember there are other options available to you in the form of temporary hair. For instance, if you are going to an event and you want some length, then buy some clip-in hair extensions and add to it.

Q. What advice would you give brides-to-be with regard to caring for their hair so that it looks its best on their big day?

M O'K It's very important to have a trial before your wedding. Don't have your trial too far in advance because your hair will change. On the other hand, you shouldn't leave it too close to the wedding either because you may keep changing your mind about the kind of style you want, five or six weeks before the wedding is the perfect timeframe. You need to forget about what you normally do with your hair because this is a totally different and new experience. Some women might say, "I never wear my hair up, so I want it down for my wedding." It might look lovely worn loose, but when you have the dress and veil on, it might not work so well. You need to think about the whole look. You have to remember that you wouldn't normally wear a wedding dress or a veil so you need to think differently when it comes to your hairstyle as well. It's all about the package – the dress, the make-up and the hair – and how the whole look comes together. A hairstylist will usually have a strong feeling about the kind of hairstyle the bride will like. Sometimes, they're right; other times they're wrong, but that's what trials are all about – trying out different looks. It's important for the bride to bring in the accessories, such as the veil or headpiece that she will be wearing on the day.

Q. What hairstyling advice would you offer to men?

GK   Most men are very clued in when it comes to products. In fact, in my opinion, men are more vain than women! The dry hair look is very in-style at the moment. Instead of using wet-look gels, opt for hair wax products. Most guys are concerned with hair loss but a great remedy is to massage your scalp regularly with your fingers as this will keep the blood flowing. Even scratching your head for five minutes will stimulate your scalp! There are also a variety of products available to combat hair loss. I have been using the same shampoo for years. It's called Prevention and it keeps the scalp really clean and free from a build-up of product which is really important for men.

The cleaner the scalp, the longer you will hold on to your hair!

Q. Given that a lot of strong hairsprays tend to either drag the hair down or give it that straw-like look, could you offer any other tips on how to make curls last longer? Secondly, how damaging is hairspray to the hair?

GK   I'm a great advocate of using the product before you're finished. In other words, if you use a good blow-drying lotion (not mousse because this can be very drying on the hair), then use it before you get to the hairspray stage. There are hundreds of blow-drying lotions on the market, it just means experimenting until you find the right one for you. Don't use too much product either; always hold the product about eighteen inches away from your hair and then lightly spray it all over. Comb the product through, then blow dry. If you get it right, then you will need very little hairspray afterwards. The thing about hairspray is that it is great if you don't want to hair to move but the moment you try to move, it's like a wire nest. It takes away the natural look. I'm not opposed to hairspray, I just think it's better to use a product before the blow-drying stage in order to get results.

Lisa's
Style Guide

Invitation Translation

DECIPHERING THE DREADED DRESS CODE

If you want to send someone into a frazzle, hand them an invitation with a dress code they don't understand.

Such a seemingly simple thing can induce an alarming amount of stress and panic in unsuspecting guests. After all, does the term 'semi-formal' mean the men can wear suits, or would such a garment be considered 'formal wear'? Should they wear jeans and a blazer or would that be seen as 'casual wear'?

Every time I think about the litany of questions these invitation terms bring about, my blood pressure swiftly rises to almost dangerous proportions. If only for the good of our health, I felt it necessary to devise an 'invitation translation' section for the book!

Invitation terms

Formal dress codes

Black tie

A black-tie dress code can mean only one thing: floor-length evening gown for the women and a tuxedo with a white shirt, cufflinks and a tie or bow-tie for the men.

A friend of mine employs a brilliant technique whenever she finds herself in doubt over whether her choice of outfit constitutes as 'black-tie'. She asks herself the following question: 'Would I wear this outfit if I were meeting the president?'

Black tie optional/black tie invited

With this particular dress code, men have the option of wearing a dark suit or a tuxedo, while women have the choice of a gown, cocktail dress or suit.

Creative black tie

This dress code is the same as black tie but allows you the opportunity to be more creative and daring with your black tie attire, headpieces or tiaras. It's usually a good idea to double check with the host on this one.

Evening dress

If your invitation stipulates 'evening dress', then elegance is what you need to look for in a garment. 'Evening dress' is basically dressier than formal wear but not as dressy as black-tie.

Formal

Depending on the type of event you are attending, formal attire can mean tuxedos or sharp dark suits for men, and long gowns or elegant cocktail dresses for women. For men, a dark suit paired with a white shirt and dark tie is always a winner.

Semi-formal
(also known as cocktail dress)

'Semi-formal' has caused many a headache in its time.

The term basically means that tuxedos and floor-length gowns are not required. For semi-formal evening events, guests should wear dark suits or short stylish dresses (aim for a knee-length hemline). For semi-formal daytime events, men can wear light-coloured suits or dark suits with bright shirts. When the dress code dictates semi-formal, the key is to aim for stylish rather than glitzy.

Informal

To begin, 'informal' does not mean 'casual'. When the host stipulates that you dress 'informally', ask them to specify whether they mean 'smart casual' or 'cocktail' as the term can mean either. If it is a particularly special event, then men should wear a dark suit while women should wear a short, elegant dress.

Cocktail dress

This essentially means short/knee-length dresses. The good thing about this particular dress code is that you are not limited in terms of dress styles. Whether you want to wear a little black dress or a colourful number, the choice is entirely yours.

Eva Longoria

Casual dress codes

Casual

This does not mean sloppy, it means comfortable clothing appropriate to the setting of the event. Jeans or khakis paired with a nice top will work just fine.

Smart casual

For this look, you are aiming for an outfit that is informal yet smart. For example, men should wear jeans and a long-sleeve shirt, while woman should wear something along the lines of a blazer and a crisp shirt over jeans or, if they prefer, a skirt and top. Black and grey trousers will also work with most items to give you the smart casual look.

Dressy casual

'Dressy casual' is very similar to 'smart casual' as it calls for a dressed-up version of your casual look. Although it depends greatly on the kind of event you are attending, jeans do not usually qualify as dressy casual. If you do want to wear jeans, however, try to go for the darkest shade possible. A wrap dress is ideal for this dress code.

Business dress codes

Business standard

For a man, this dress code would imply that he wear a sharp suit and tie. For a woman, a pencil skirt with a smart shirt is appropriate.

Business formal

Business formal carries most of the same rules as the semi-formal dress code – dark, tailored suits for men and sharp, stylish suits/dresses for women.

Business casual

A blazer worn over dark jeans will do the job nicely when the dress code is business casual. If you prefer to wear a suit, don't wear a tie. The main thing to remember is that you should still look professional.

Always remember...

Regardless of the dress code, the number one rule when choosing an outfit for a party remains the same: *Never upstage the hostess!*

Tyra Banks works the 'business formal' style.

ASK THE EXPERT...
BARRY MCCALL,
FASHION
PHOTOGRAPHER

Q. How should a woman pose for a camera?

A. First of all, I would suggest that you stand at a slight angle to the camera rather than facing it straight on. By standing at an angle, you are narrowing your silhouette. Another tip, albeit one you have to be careful with, involves very slightly lowering your chin so that you're placing the emphasis on your eyes as well as narrowing your jaw line. Lastly, don't try to hold the same smile for ten seconds or more because it will only end up looking unnatural. Relax your face for a moment and then return with a fresh look.

Q. When posing, should a woman place her hands – behind her back, on her hip, etc?

A. I have seen a great posing technique used by some people where they place something small like a coin in their hands and it's as though their fingers are slightly playing with it. Sometimes the hand-on-the-hip pose can appear quite formal, whereas the coin-in-the-hand trick offers a more relaxed look. Never pose with a drink in your hand. No matter what event you are at, move the glass to one side and pose without it.

Q. Do people pay enough attention to their posture when it comes to photographs?

A. I heard a great tip from the wonderful Maureen O'Hara when I worked with her on a shoot recently. She had been using the term

'B-I-C-O' and when I asked her what it was, she replied, 'Belly in, chest out.' I thought that was pretty good advice!

Posture wise, don't stand bolt upright, but make sure you're not slouching either. If the camera is facing you directly, then move one-third of an angle to your left or right while all the time keeping your face towards the camera.

Q. When posing for a photograph, women sometimes choose to pout rather than smile, primarily because they feel it's sexier. However, as a fashion photographer, do you think women look better smiling?

A. When a person looks at a photograph, they generally want to see people smiling and enjoying themselves rather than looking pouty and standoffish. Models pout in magazines because they are trying to express a particular mood, but in ordinary photographs, you should be seen as approachable and at your friendliest.

When photographing a model for a shoot, there is a way of helping us establish the kind of smile that will suit her. There are essentially three types of smiles, but it's all to do with the mouth shape, so to determine which of the three will suit the model, I get her to say 'ha-ha-ha', then 'he-he-he' and lastly 'ho-ho-ho'.

Naturally, you won't be able to do this every time your photograph is being taken, however, it is a good way to help you decide which kind of smile best suits you.

Q. What pose can a woman adopt to disguise a double chin?

A. There are so many different factors that would have to be taken into consideration here, such as which way the woman is being photographed, if there is a flash being used or if she is being photographed inside or outside. A general suggestion I would have would be to tilt your chin slightly (around half an inch) so that the emphasis is on your jaw line, your eyes and your mouth. This should take the attention away from your chin. Sometimes when I ask a model to tilt her chin, you can see the skin being slightly squashed around the neck, so I rectify this by getting her to do some relaxing exercises such as rolling her neck. If you feel as though your skin is being squashed, then just relax your neck before returning to the pose.

Q. When it comes to wedding photography, what specifics should a couple look for when choosing a photographer?

A. Carry out as much research on your photographer as you would on your dress or your hotel. It's a good idea to also go through wedding magazines and take note of the different styles that you like and the names of the photographers responsible for them. Wedding planners would also be able to recommend good photographers. When you have narrowed down your list of potential photographers arrange a meeting and have them show you a variety of work they have done. If you find a photographer you like, run their name by places such as hotels and wedding planners. Find out as much as you can before making your final decision.

Celebrity red carpet tips

- If you are conscious of your weight, never pose for a photograph with your hands down by your side. This will only add to the illusion of width and will make you appear heavier. Always make sure there is some space between your body and your arm. This particular pose will also make your arms and shoulders appear leaner.

- If you have a habit of blinking just as the flash goes off, then ask the photographer to count down from three before taking the picture. Keep your eyes closed until they reach number one. When you open your eyes, you will be just in time for the flash. At last, no more closed eyes in photographs!

- When posing for a photograph with two friends, stand slightly back in the centre with your friends standing slightly forward at your left and right sides. This will give you a narrow silhouette.

- For full-length photographs, place one foot in front of the other (make sure your toe is pointing towards the camera) and top it off by placing your hands confidently on your hips. This helps create the illusion of longer legs and make you look leaner. If you don't feel confident enough to carry off this pose, then try slightly crossing your legs instead.

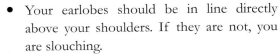

Penelope Cruz works the simple hand-on-the-hip pose.

- Your earlobes should be in line directly above your shoulders. If they are not, you are slouching.

- If you are having your photograph taken when you are sat down, then make sure you are sitting towards the edge of the seat. This will help you appear leaner. You should also move your body so that your hip is angled towards the camera and that your legs are crossed. Be careful not to cross your legs at the knee, however, as your calf muscle will appear bigger.

- For a casual relaxed pose, place your thumb in your belt loophole, tilt your head and, while keeping both feet in line, very slightly bend one leg so that your hip is at an angle.

Eva Longoria

PAUL COSTELLOE, DESIGNER

"Paul Costelloe's down-to-earth clothes look magnificent!"
Liza Minnelli

Ask most designers why they became involved in fashion and they will immediately launch into tales of their love affair with sketching magnificent creations, their lofty ambitions to be the kind of designer that every woman wants to wear, and their big plans to change the face of fashion worldwide.

Put the same question to Irish designer Paul Costelloe and, without hesitation, he will tell you that his love of fashion stems primarily from an appreciation for dressing real women. He likes people who "don't take fashion too seriously" and prefers to see his designs being worn by ordinary women on the street than those who populate the catwalk.

Where most designers like to grace the social pages as much as they do the fashion pages, Paul has become famous for shunning the celebrity lifestyle that centres around premières, parties and pretence.

After thirty-one years in the fashion business, he remains an industry heavyweight. So when it came to garnering expert advice on all things style, he certainly wasn't in short supplying answers!

159

Q. Paul you were very much a rugby player growing up, so where did your career in fashion begin?

A. Because of my academic failings, it was with very little choice that I got into the fashion career. I attended Blackrock College and when I left, my options were painting, design, something of that nature; a career that didn't require anything like mathematics or English. Luckily, I was encouraged in school to paint and, as time went on, I fell into fashion more and more. Following a year studying in Grafton Academy, I travelled to Paris and walked its beautiful streets. I suppose I lived a fairly nomadic style of life and learned what I could along the way. Back in the late 1960s and early 1970s, Paris was the place to be, but Milan has since eclipsed Paris. I always moved around, New York, London, Paris, Milan, but I stuck with design and learned from other people. I survived from there!

Q. At what point did you decide you could develop your own brand?

A. My strength was in materials, which I've always believed was a gift from God. You can't teach textiles. I think people recognised that I had a certain identity; there weren't very many of us in the industry back then and, even today, there still aren't that many in Ireland – it's the same names that always keep cropping up.

Luckily, I was born with a good name; I didn't have to change it to a stronger one. I developed the fox logo because I related to hunting and foxes. I continued the logo throughout the collection and I retained it even in England around the time of the anti-hunting controversy. I feel as though I'm bit of a fox myself in that I always hang around the outside! Foxes always walk in the shadows and I think I'm quite like that.

Q. Where do you find your inspiration for your designs?

A. Deadlines! When you have a deadline, you have no choice but to come up with something. For instance, my collection in early 2010 was inspired by the movie *The Assassination of Jesse James*; a great movie starring Brad Pitt. My instinctive design is natural, understated, relaxed and not too uptight. I firmly believe that people should enjoy wearing clothes and not take them too seriously. That has always been my attitude. I like people who are not overly dependent on fashion.

Q. Classic tailoring like yours is so elegant. It has amazing longevity and is completely trend resistant. Would you advise women to save up and buy quality key pieces rather than splurging on trends that come and go?

A. I totally agree with investing in quality clothes. In Italy and France, it's in their culture to do that, but unfortunately it's not a habit we have in the UK and Ireland. We tend to look for instant gratification rather than investing in pieces that will last. I don't see our attitude as being totally wrong either though. I like the idea of mixing high street with designer. With a lot of the high street brands, the quality is very good. If you are young then mixing high street and designer can look great. However, if you are that bit older – even if you have the figure for it – it won't look that good.

Q. Given your penchant for fabrics, can you tell us the best ones to pack when travelling?

A. In winter, the best fabric is wool because it doesn't wrinkle. In spring, I think it's good to have a blend of fabrics. Some of the man-made fibres are very good for when you are travelling – for example, a blend of viscose or silk.

The word polyester sounds awful but it's actually very sophisticated and it does perform. It also looks great and, to be honest, people can't tell the difference any more. Silk is quite good but it's hard to maintain. Linen is also a very beautiful fibre but, again, very difficult. Linen jerseys in particular are quite good and they are also very comfortable.

Q. At what age should a woman stop wearing revealing necklines?

A. I personally think discretion is the best advice regardless of a woman's age. From a male perspective, the less that's on display, the better. The less we see, the more exciting it is! The fit and the shape of the clothes will make you look attractive, not the amount of flesh you can show. Women might feel differently but, from the male point of view, it's far more exciting and much more appealing when a woman doesn't have everything on display.

Q. Everyone has their own theory on what fashion means to them. How would you define the word 'fashion'?

A. It's the life of the moment we are living in. It can reflect anything from our economy to how we feel within ourselves; whether we're comfortable or uncomfortable, happy or unhappy.

Yes what you wear can sometimes provoke misconceptions about who you are but that's fine because that's the fun of being a woman. Women have the joy of using fashion to be multifaceted. Men are very different, however – we reflect one image regardless of whether its morning, noon or night! We're very consistent!

Q. What is it about the Aran Islands that inspires your designs and sketches?

A. The Aran Islands inspire my paintings more so than my fashion sketches. It's a place that is so extremely different. Milan is where I gained my experience, my love for fashion and the encouragement to continue no matter

Less is more – skip the plunging neckline and go for the plunging backline like Bette Davis.

what, but the Aran Islands is where I can just be me. I'm a father of seven children. Trying to get the balance with both work and family is very important, but it's difficult as fashion can absorb so much of your time. You are constantly on the move. The Aran Islands however, for me, is a place of such great peace. I know and love many people there. I was the youngest of a large family and being on the islands takes me back to my basic upbringing, and the loneliness that can sometimes come with being part of a large family.

Q. What's the one mistake women make time and time again when it comes to style?

A. Number one mistake is buying clothes that are too tight. It might look ok at the front but then you see how tight it is at the back and you just think, Why not buy one size up? Don't worry if it's a size fourteen or sixteen. Every manufacturer has a different take on sizing. What might be a size twelve for one manufacturer is a size eight for another. There's no standardised size so don't dwell on it. Another mistake women make is buying shoes with heels that are too high. They can't walk in them and when they try, you can see their ankles going left and right! It looks ridiculous.

Q. What matters most to you as a fashion designer? Does it infuriate you to see someone who has it all wrong in terms of fashion?

A. Oh God, no! I get ideas from looking at how people wear their clothes and how great different items look on them. Above all, when I'm designing, I think it's important to get

into the mood of the kind of person who will be wearing my clothes. I have an imaginary woman in my head and she's the individual whom I picture my customer being.

Q. What advice would you offer to people who are considering pursing a career in fashion?

A. Work with established people first. Don't just decide that you are going to quit college and start up your own label. If you can, get your training and college experience in Italy. It's exceptionally good there because they train people from such a young age. Tokyo (and Japan in general) is also wonderful and have very high standards in their design schools.

If you feel that you can't it make in design, then try retail, but always remember, it's never going to be a nine to five job!

Q. What is your favourite part of the design process?

A. I love the very early stages. From the design stage to the garment stage, or the muslin stage where you can draw on the poplin and make all the necessary changes. Throughout those stages I am working with a qualified pattern person, which is great because those kind of people are in very short supply, especially in England and Ireland.

Q. You must be very proud when you look at a new collection hanging on the clothes rails? You are literally looking at the creations that were once sketches!

A. No, I only see the mistakes! I might see a fit problem or I might question why a garment was made in a certain way. It's a team process. The clothes might be made in a different country or somewhere very far away from your base, and it can be difficult to control it and to get it back in the right image that you anticipated. Painting is a lot easier!

Q. Who is the one person you would like to give a makeover to?

A. Michelle Obama.

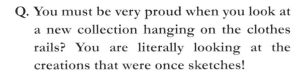

1. Jodie Kidd with Paul Costelloe
2. Caprice
3. Jerry Hall

163

Holiday Fashion

HOLIDAY PACKING

If the thought of packing for a holiday is almost enough to put you off the idea of going away, then you will be pleased to hear that your pre-holiday stress is about to reach an abrupt end.

I don't know of one woman, myself included, who hasn't been guilty of over-packing. We all begin with good intentions of packing only the necessities but then we find our eyes slowly wandering over to that dress we bought a week earlier and suddenly we think, I'll bring it just in case. A quick bout of panic soon sets in and we decide we have to bring along a pair of heels in every colour so that we will be covered for all situations. Before we know it, a dozen more items are going on holiday with the dress.

Travel light? Impossible!

Or so we think.

Even Marlene Dietrich
struggled with holiday packing!

- Before you begin packing, think about what you plan to do for the week. Do you intend to go out every night? Will you be on the beach every day or will you be travelling a lot? When you outline the specifics, it makes it easier to decide which items to pack.

- If you are holidaying for two weeks, pack enough for one week. There is absolutely no reason why you can't wear the same outfit twice. What's more, changing your accessories can make any outfit look completely different.

- Don't pack the outfits as you choose them. Lay them all out on the bed first so that you can see exactly what you plan to bring and which items can be paired together to create new looks. If you pack them directly into your suitcase, you will be tempted to sneak in a variety of just-in-case items.

- Remember, the more colourful the clothes you pack, the more difficult it will be to mix and match. Instead you can inject colour into your holiday style through accessories.

- Forget pearls and diamonds! Be adventurous with your jewellery when on holiday. Wear bold and bright colourful pieces.

- Roll your clothes when packing. Not only will you fit more items in your suitcase this way, you will also have crease-free clothes when you unpack.

- Don't wear a black beach hat if you are holidaying in a very warm climate. Black absorbs heat and will increase your chances of sunburn.

Rita Hayworth

- Bring a white dress and two or three colourful shawls. You can wear the dress with a beach hat during the day and, at night, pair it with a shawl will give an elegant, dressy look. Wedges will work for both day and night.

- Depending on whether or not you are going on a snow or sunshine holiday, you should always pack a key item (such as linen trousers or jeans) that you can wear with a variety of tops.

- Bring one evening dress. Wear it either on its own or with a cardigan one evening, and then pair it with a wrap when you wear it on another evening.

- If you are going on a sun holiday, tops or dresses with prints always look amazing in the sunshine. You can never go wrong with a floral summer dress.

- When choosing which items to pack, pay attention to the fabrics. Which ones will travel well? If you are travelling to a hot climate, will the fabric cling to your skin and make you feel clammy? Will it show up perspiration stains? Select clothing that allows your skin to breathe. Cotton and linen are wonderful fabrics for hot climates.

- Leave the short shorts to the teenagers. Instead keep it classy and wear A-line skirts instead.

- The outfit you wear when travelling to your holiday destination can double up as your return-journey attire.

1.

2.

3.

- Avoid maxi dresses unless you are tall. You need to be of a certain height to successfully carry off this look.

- Holidays are all about comfort so leave your high heels at home! Flip flops and wedges are holiday necessities. For evening events, bring a pair of silver or gold sandals.

- While Capri pants are a fantastic addition to a holiday wardrobe, steer clear of them if you are petite and would like to look taller. If however you are happy with your height, wear them proudly!

- Kaftans are wonderful to wear on the beach if you are conscious of your weight.

1. As Kylie Minogue proves, jeans are wonderful for a causal chic look and are one of the most versatile items to bring with you on holiday.
2. At five foot eight inches tall, Paris Hilton can carry off the maxi look.
3. Flip-flop fan Nicole Ritchie.

- In terms of accessories, think neutral. Look at your clothes and ask yourself which handbag/hair accessories will go with almost everything? Space is not a luxury offered to us by our suitcases so forget packing one in every colour.

- Silver, white or black will usually go with everything. Jewellery and headscarves are the exception to the rule as they take up minimal space.

- Don't forget to pack the correct underwear, e.g. nude bra for under white dress.

- When packing swimwear, don't forget the staple accessories such as sunglasses, sun cream and a sarong.

- Reserve a pocket in your handbag for important travel documents including your passport, travel insurance, hotel details and boarding pass.. Doing this will prevent that dreaded last-minute panic.

Stars with airport style

1. Cheryl Cole
2. Angelina Jolie
3. Gisele Bundchen
4. Catherine Zeta Jones
5. Cameron Diaz

LISA TIPS... FOR TRAVELLING

Dirty laundry

People will often pack a plastic bag in their suitcase for dirty laundry however, as we all know only too well, it's never big enough or strong enough. A much better solution is to use an old pillowcase. It won't take up any room in your case when neatly folded.

No more plane hair

If your hair tends to go limp or oily during a long flight, bring along a bottle of dry shampoo. This will inject your hair with volume when you need it most.

Wonder oil

The one product every traveller should own is Jojoba oil. Its versatility makes it the ideal handbag companion as it can be used as a moisturiser for both your face and skin, as well as a leave-in conditioner or smoothing balm for your hair. It works particularly well on hair that reacts to humidity.

Substitution!

Don't give valuable space in your suitcase to unnecessary items. Instead of bringing shaving cream for example, use your hair conditioner to acquire that smooth clean shave. Its thick texture makes it an ideal substitute.

Hair conditioner is just as effective as shaving cream for keeping your legs smooth.

Your Wedding

I have to admit, I love wedding traditions. When it came to my own wedding, I turned up more than just a bit late, but this had less to do with tradition and more to do with us deliberately taking a longer journey to the church. You see, every time I saw a bride on her way to the church, I always sounded the car horn. But when I was being driven to the church, there wasn't a car horn to be heard! Feeling a bit put out by this, I asked the chauffeur to drive us back around the block again with the strict instruction that he noise the horn at other drivers to encourage a reaction from them! When I ended up being somewhat late for the ceremony, I did what all brides do and blamed tradition!

When it comes to your wedding, your grand entrance should be the one and only task you leave to the last minute! Believe me, a little organisation in the early days will spare you a considerable amount of stress in the long run. To help you on your way, I have compiled a month by month wedding plan which you will find at the end of this section!

Girls, don't allow yourself to become overwhelmed by the enormity of the event and, above all, don't feel as though you have to oversee every task personally. Have the confidence to reach out and ask for assistance. Believe me, there are plenty of people in your life who would only be delighted to help out in the preparations!

In the run up to my wedding, I really came to appreciate the little tips that were offered to me by friends who had already been through the experience. One such tip concerned my arrival at the church aisle. As anyone who has been there will know, the moment you step into the church, you immediately hear everyone shuffling to turn around and look at you. You're wearing the dress; the flowers in the church are arranged just how you asked; the man of your dreams is waiting for you at the alter, and, at that moment, your emotions are running so high that you realise you could burst into tears with excitement. Fortunately, a good friend had earlier advised me to smile the moment I heard people shuffling to turn around. When you do this, the emotion transforms into excitement rather than tears and you don't end up ruining your make-up!

Over the years, I have worked at many wedding seminars, and through emails to my website, I have answered hundreds of questions from brides-to-be. I think at this stage I could probably write a book on wedding advice alone! For the moment, I'm going to stick to talking about one of the favourite features of a wedding day: The Dress!

TIPS TO CONSIDER BEFORE BUYING YOUR DRESS

Dress styles

When it comes to finding the style that best suits your shape, there is no substitute for going into the bridal boutiques and actively trying on the various different gowns. Don't forget to bring a few essential items to help you get a feel for the completed look.

To help you on your way, here is a brief summary of dress styles.

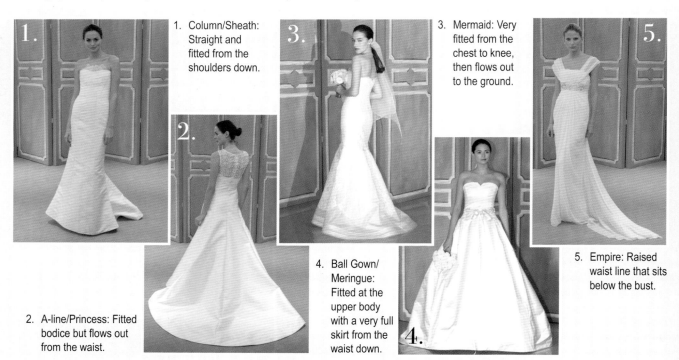

1. Column/Sheath: Straight and fitted from the shoulders down.

2. A-line/Princess: Fitted bodice but flows out from the waist.

3. Mermaid: Very fitted from the chest to knee, then flows out to the ground.

4. Ball Gown/Meringue: Fitted at the upper body with a very full skirt from the waist down.

5. Empire: Raised waist line that sits below the bust.

"Mummy's fairy dress!"

When I was shopping for my wedding dress, it seemed like wonderful luck that I fell madly in love with the first gown I tried on. Unfortunately, however, my luck was out when it came to the gown's price tag as it cost almost a mortgage to buy. I decided there and then that a crafty plan would be necessary if my dream wedding dress was going to share my big day. While we were in the dressing room, I had my friend take some photographs of me wearing the dress (some may call it cheeky – I prefer to call it initiative!) Later, when we returned home, she sketched some designs of the dress in question. We then brought our photographs and artwork to Brid Nihill and had the exact same gown made for a third of the price. Believe me, girls, it pays to be creative!

I know people will argue that some brides lavish too much attention (and money) on their dress, and in a way, they are right. Regardless of how you look at it however, the dress will always be the masterpiece of the day. It's your one day to feel like royalty and, when you think about it, most people will ask you about the dress before they'll ask you about the venue. My advice, though, is to keep the gown a secret.

I refused to reveal any details about my dress. In fact, the only person who saw it before the wedding day was the friend who helped me photograph it in the dressing room! In the end, it became such a secret that it turned out to be a really big surprise on the day itself. My reasons for keeping the dress details secret are the same as those behind not giving away the name you have chosen for your baby when you're pregnant. This was a great piece of advice given to me by a friend which I now regret not having heeded at the time.

My friend had advised me not to tell people the name we had chosen for our first born because if one person said they didn't like the name or made a face at the mention of it, it would more than likely be enough to turn us off the name we had chosen. Take this same approach with your wedding dress – don't give anyone any details. If asked, just explain that it's a surprise. That way, there will be an amazing build up to your church entrance because everyone will be waiting in anticipation to see you in your beautiful gown.

Don't forget about post-wedding care. I decided to have my dress vacuum packed as it is the best way to preserve the material and colour. Though the other main method for storing clothing is boxed in acid-free paper (you can buy museum-quality boxes for the best storage).

It's nice to hold on to all those kinds of memory, particularly if you go on to have children as it is something you will enjoy showing them in years to come. I plan to cut open the seal on the vacuum pack when my daughter Sophie is old enough to really appreciate the dress. For now, though, she's happy to look at the photos and refer to it as "Mummy's fairy dress".

Lisa on her wedding day.

Tips to consider when shopping for your dress

- You will always find the dress of your dreams so don't panic if your search doesn't yield results straight away. If you can't find 'the one' in the bridal shops, then hire a seamstress to make it for you.

  There are so many shops with such a phenomenal selection of dresses but, there are also many people out there who are highly skilled in designing and creating the dress of your dreams. If you have a specific vision of a dress in mind, rest assured that there are always ways of making it a reality.

- Know your budget and stick to it. You will only be wearing this dress for one day so don't obsess over labels. No one will know if it's not designer.

- When you meet with the sales assistant, let them know your price range. If they keep showing you items that are out of your range, go elsewhere.

- When you find your dream dress, take down the relevant information such as the name of the designer and the serial number. Search for the dress online and see if there are stockists who are selling it at a cheaper price. If you don't shop around, it may cost you dearly.

- Think about the jewellery that will best suit your shade of gown. Diamante is beautiful with a white dress, while pearls are stunning with an ivory dress. Simplicity is the key to wedding beauty. If you are wearing a diamante tiara, then avoid wearing a blingy necklace and earrings. Have one key piece but make sure your other pieces are toned down considerably.

- Don't feel limited to wearing white on your wedding day. Try on champagne, ivory and gold wedding gowns as they may be far more flattering against your skin tone.

- There is so much available in terms of hair accessories for the bride. A veil is a beautiful tradition however if you are not planning on having one, then shops such as Claire's Accessories have a wonderful selection of inexpensive decorative clips while shops like Accesorize have beautiful headpieces. There is also a large range of inexpensive tiaras out there for brides to avail of. It's only when you shop around that you begin to spot such wonderful deals.

TANNING

If you are having a tan, it's a good idea to have it applied three days before your wedding. That way, you are giving yourself ample time to correct any mistakes or to have a top-up if necessary. It's not uncommon for brides to take a holiday before the wedding so that they can sit out in the sun and obtain a natural tan. When they return home, however, you can often see the marks of their bra straps! If you are planning the 'tanning trip', ensure that you remove the bra straps so that you are not left with any lines. No amount of fake tan will cover the marks left behind by the straps – and I assure, you they will show up in photographs. For more advice and key tips on achieving the perfect tan, go to page 137.

Bridal footwear

- Buy your shoes in good time before your final fitting so that your dress can be altered to suit the level of the shoe. Sometimes dressmakers have a tendency to go an inch longer, but I find it's not worth it and you certainly don't notice it in photographs. You don't want to be tripping over your dress and then having to pick it up when you're dancing, so, to avoid this problem, have your dress altered so that it's resting just above the base of your foot. If it kick-flairs out as you walk, then you know you're not going to trip over it.

- Go for a shoe with an ankle strap. They are so comfortable and much easier to get around in. Forget high heels! You will be working the room for lengthy periods of time, not to mention dancing the night away. Do you really want high-heel induced foot pain to ruin your first dance?

- A week before the wedding, wear your shoes around the house. This will help you get used to them and break them in.

Ankle-strap bridal shoes.

ASK THE EXPERT: TARA FAY, XENA PRODUCTIONS

If you're planning your dream party, then Tara Fay is the woman you will want at the helm. Having trained with a leading events company in Los Angeles, Tara returned to Ireland where she established her own company, Xena Productions, in 1997. This was the first event company in Ireland to specialise in the organisation of events and weddings and, since its formation, Tara and her team have been responsible for some of the most glamorous weddings in showbusiness.

In January 2010, Tara was presented with a Gala award, the Oscar equivalent in the Special Events Industry, for 'the best wedding in 2009'. Xena Productions now hold the prestigious record of being the first European company ever to take home this accolade. 'Weddings by Tara Fay' have featured in all the Irish wedding magazines, *Brides* in the UK, *Victoria* magazine in the USA and also *Hello* magazine worldwide. Tara is also highly sought after as a speaker for event and wedding seminars throughout the country and regularly lectures to students. She is currently Chairperson of the Irish Chapter of the International Special Events Society and is country co-ordinator for the Association of Bridal Consultants in Ireland.

I have seen Tara in action and the word 'amazing' immediately comes to my mind to describe the way she works. There's no running, no mayhem, but you just know that everything is happening as it should and that all is going according to plan.

The one thing I notice about Tara is that she is always observing; making sure everything is on time and that everyone is happy. No small detail is left unnoticed or ignored. I remember one night, Tara noticed a lady putting on her jacket as she was cold. Immediately, she set about rectifying the situation, checking to see if the lady was sitting in the pathway of an open air vent. When you see Tara in action, she is the personification of professionalism. Even though her mind may be juggling everything that's going on, she is the face of calm. As such, I couldn't think of anyone better to provide us with answers to those frequently asked wedding questions!

Q. Weddings are inevitably going to be expensive, but can you offer any money-saving ideas that might help reduce the cost in some areas?

A. A good wedding planner should help you to not spend money foolishly. They should actually help you save money – in fact a planner's fee should be almost equal to the amount of money you have saved because of the advice they have given you. For instance, I plan around fifteen weddings each year and over the course of my fourteen years in the business, I have built up relationships with different suppliers. As a result, I can acquire discounts and good deals for couples that they would not have been able to get by themselves. Again, it's about helping the couple to spend their money wisely. Similarly, if they want something specific, I can direct them to the person who will do it best.

It's important for couples to set out a budget for the day. Second to buying a house, your wedding day is the most expensive investment you are going to make. Decide what you want and if it's achievable within your budget. If it's not, look at the different things you can do without.

What are you willing to compromise on? For example if you always dreamed of getting married in summer but you discover its cheaper to get married in autumn, are you willing to compromise and have an autumn wedding instead?

Summer flowers are gone by August, but, if you are getting married in August or September, your flowers will be slightly cheaper because there is an abundance of them available.

Midweek weddings are usually cheaper. In fact, the royals always got married on a Wednesday. When it comes to weddings, there's a lovely saying that goes: 'Monday for wealth, Tuesday for health, Wednesday the best day of all, Thursday for losses, Friday for crosses and Saturday no luck at all.'

Around thirty or forty years ago, a lot of people got married on a Wednesday. Traders would close their shops for a half-day each Wednesday so people usually got married on that day because most of their guests would be on a half-day from work. Saturday weddings have really only become popular in the past twenty years.

Some people find it is much cheaper to get married abroad. If this is your choice, make sure your paperwork is sorted in time.

In terms of being creative on a budget, you should think outside the box. I love IKEA because you can get the most beautiful accessories and vases that make for wonderful table centrepieces. There are ways of achieving different looks without the expense. For example, when I was in the supermarket recently, I saw ten roses for something like €2.99. There are so many different ways you could use those roses. It's just all about being creative.

When I am working with a couple, I will always sit down with them and go through their budget. They will have told me what their dream wedding is, so I will show them how much that will cost. If it's outside their budget range, we then work out the things they are willing to compromise on. We cut back on the bells and whistles and come to a solution so that they can still achieve their dream wedding.

Tara's Top Tips

- The hairdresser will usually ensure that one of your bridesmaids knows how to correctly remove your veil from your hair but you should make a point of knowing how to do it too, in case the bridesmaid isn't around to help you.

- Think about what you are going to wear the day after your wedding. Remember, a lot of your guests will have stayed the night so it's always nice to look your best the following day because the attention will still be on both you and your groom.

- So many couples panic about the first dance. Some people like it, others don't. It's a personal choice. Some people prefer to have guests up dancing for fifteen to twenty minutes and then do their first dance. Go with whatever you are comfortable with.

- When sourcing a photographer, hire one who is a member of IPPA because they will be covered by IPPA insurance. A good photographer will be creative and capture the special moments. They might seem expensive, but, remember, you are paying for their experience and their expertise. You want someone who knows all about the proper lighting for photographs and who can position people in a way that works well for group shots. You are paying for their experience in the job.

- Couples often get freaked out by the invitation list. The main reason for this is that they don't appreciate how long it takes to gather names and addresses. At the very beginning of the planning process, I always send clients a spreadsheet and tell them to begin filling it out right away. It's often the case that couples suddenly realise that they don't actually know the names of their relations' spouses.

Q. What hidden costs and stipulations should couples remember to ask about when planning their wedding (e.g. churches that have a strict policy on music and flowers)?

A. Churches that have been refurbished sometimes don't like candles in certain places so it's always a good idea to check beforehand. If you want to stick something up in the church, use Blue-tac – never ever use nails or Sellotape, which will pull off the paint. Try instead to tie things in place. Each church is different and you will basically need to check what may or may not be allowed. It could be church policy not to allow something or it might be insurance related. Even the songs you play at your wedding might be restricted. The Catholic Church has produced a list of liturgically correct music and some churches will make you choose from that list.

When I worked on a wedding in Spain last year, we had to change a beautiful piece of classical music because the sacristan decided he didn't like one of the lines in the music. I had an ecumenical debate with him about it and explained that we were not using the words, just the music itself, but he still wouldn't allow it.

Q. Can you outline the exact role of a wedding planner?

A. When outlining my role, I always tell my clients to envision their wedding as a theatre production and to look at a wedding planner as the stage manager. The bride and groom, however, are the directors. It's not a wedding planner's role to come in and take over a wedding. A planner is there to help, assist and guide the couple through the whole process.

Often people don't know what they want when it comes to their wedding, but they usually know what they don't want, so I try to go through their likes and dislikes and build a picture of what will work for them.

Before we even begin looking at venues or churches, I try to find out more about the couple's respective personalities. Everyone has their own tastes and a wedding should be a reflection of that individuality. It's very important to get the groom involved in the planning and to find out his preferences as well. If a couple are unsure about what they want, I will usually talk to them about other weddings they have attended and get them to tell me what features they liked or disliked about those weddings. On the other hand, it might be a wedding scene in a movie that grabbed their attention. I might ask them if they liked the church scene from *Friends* where Ross and Emily got married in a rundown church covered in fairy lights and candles. We establish what they couple would like to have and then look into the various options and ideas in that area. When we have established the groundwork, we can move forward.

Q. Often couples feel under pressure from their families to invite the distant relations and various people that neither the bride nor groom may be very familiar with. As this is often a subject of stress for couples, how should they deal with it?

A. Are the people in question on your Christmas card list? If not, then think twice about inviting them. If your guest list is bigger than you anticipated, revise it. With some names, you will have to ask yourself, 'Do I really want them there? Do I need to have them there? What will be the calamity if I don't invite them?'

When you open the door for one, you will end up probably having to invite ten more. Some people might shrug it off and say 'but its only ten extra guests', but that actually means ten couples so really its twenty guests. This will mean ten more invitations and ten lots of postage. You will also have to order ten more mass booklets. If you have little wedding favours for the guests, you now have to pay for twenty more. For the reception, you will have to add on two extra tables and pay for two more table centrepieces. If you are paying an average of €65 a head for the reception, it won't just be €650 for the ten people, it will be closer to €1,300 or more, if most of them bring partners. When you see how it all adds up, you realise that 'just ten more guests' can actually be quite expensive. That's why you have to really consider who you want there.

Q. What advice would you offer in relation to the recording aspects of the wedding?

A. Some people are unsure about whether or not they want a video of their wedding. However, it's the one thing I always encourage couples to have. Think about it. From the time you walk into the church to the time you leave, you won't remember a thing. The ceremony will fly by and it will more than likely be a blur. It's always nice to look back on the video and see your guests arriving at the church. In a few years' time, some of those people might not be around, so it's always nice to be able to look back on footage of those you love enjoying your big day.

Q. How far in advance should a bride begin searching for a wedding dress?

A. Brides should begin looking for their dress around six to eight months before the wedding. Sometimes bridal shops will put pressure on brides and say they need a sixteen-week lead-time for ordering.

Do not collect your dress until the week before the wedding. If you bring your dress home with you months before the wedding, you will keep looking at it and trying it on and, before you know it, you're bored with it.

I know brides who got fed up with their dress because they collected it too soon and they ended up going off and buying a different one. In fact, some brides I have worked with have gone through two and three dresses.

Q. How late should the bride arrive at the church?

A. Ten to fifteen minutes is the appropriate time to be late. With some very popular churches, there might be weddings at one o'clock, three o'clock and five o'clock. University Church for example is very busy and there could be two or three weddings on any given Saturday. Adare and Cratloe churches are also very popular and are often quite busy on a Saturday. In those kinds of place, you are literally allowed ten to fifteen minutes leeway. You have to be in and finished on time because when you're leaving the wedding, the guests for the next wedding are waiting outside to get in. If the bride and groom are not there on time, then the church in question can actually cancel the wedding. It might sound harsh, but they can't hold off the next scheduled wedding because you were late for yours.

Something Old, Something New . . .

Did you ever wonder why the wedding ring must be worn on the third finger of the left hand? Or perhaps why brides are suppose to have something old and something new? I really loved Tara's story about how Wednesday became the best day to get married, however the more I thought about it, the more it had me wondering about the kind of stories that lay behind our other wedding traditions.

Q. Why is the wedding ring place on the third finger of the left hand?

A. The origin of this tradition is unclear but some believe that the ring finger follows the vena amoris, the vein of love, that runs directly to the heart. By wearing your wedding ring on the third finger of the left hand, you are wearing it on the finger closest to the heart.

Q. Why do brides wear a wedding veil?

A. Some say the veil comes from a tradition associated with arranged marriages when the bride's face was covered until after the ceremony to prevent the groom from backing out if he didn't like the way she looked! Others say the veil stems from the days when it was used to protect the bride from evil spirits.

Q. Why do the guests sound their car horns when travelling behind the wedding car to the hotel?

A. It has been stated that people originally fired rifles into the air as a way of saluting the newlyweds when they passed by on their way from the church. Unfortunately this practice sometimes turned a joyful day into a tragic one. As such, the noising of car horns replaced the firing of guns.

Q. Traditionally, which days/months are seen as lucky and unlucky for a wedding?

A. An old superstition states that May is an unlucky month for a wedding because of its association with the Virgin Mary. Ironically, however, it has become one of the most popular months for weddings. It's particularly lucky to have a wedding on New Year's Eve but a wedding on Christmas Day is seen as being very unlucky.

Q. What is the significance of the phrase: "Something old, something new, something borrowed, something blue and a silver sixpence in your shoe?"

A. Something old refers to wearing something that represents a link with the bride's family and her old life, such as a piece of family jewellery.

Wearing something new represents good fortune and success in the bride's new life. For a lot of brides, the dress is usually their 'something new'. For your 'something borrowed', try to get an item that was worn by a happy bride at her wedding as this is meant to bring wonderful luck to the marriage. Wearing something blue dates back to biblical times when the colour blue was considered to represent purity and fidelity. A blue handkerchief will suffice. To place a silver sixpence (or any silver coin) in the bride's left shoe was a symbol of wealth. This is not just to bring the bride financial wealth but also a wealth of happiness and joy throughout her married life.

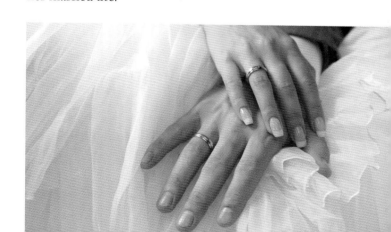

MONTH BY MONTH PLANNER

D on't allow yourself to become overwhelmed by the various tasks involved in planning a wedding. Take the following timetable as an example of how to manage the various wedding related tasks over a number of months.

Twelve to sixteen months

- Select the theme for the wedding (castle, church or outdoor ceremony). Magazines and internet sites are brilliant for generating ideas.

- Decide on your budget.

- Create a wedding folder. Use this for all things wedding related – notes, receipts, picture samples and contact details.

- Organise a guest list and have an approximate number of guests in mind before looking for a venue.

- Meet with the priest and plan the date. Prior to the meeting, choose two or three possible wedding dates. It's not unusual for venues and churches to be booked two years in advance so don't set your heart on one date as you may be setting yourself up for disappointment.

- Don't forget to discuss with the priest your selection of music and your choice of flowers too. You would be surprised how many churches have strict policies on what can and cannot be used.

- Select a venue for the wedding reception and meet with the hotel manager to book the date.

- Book your photographer and videographer.

- Choose your bridesmaids and groomsmen.

- Book your church and reception musicians as well as your DJ. Don't forget to consider whether or not you want a musician playing in the hotel lobby as the guests arrive.

- Begin the search for your dress.

Ten months

- Finalise your wedding colours and theme.

- Consider music for the church and reception.

- If you want to look your best for your big day, now is the time to begin a healthy eating and exercise programme.

Six months

- Organise rental equipment for the reception, e.g. chair covers, table covers, decorations and table centrepieces.

- Book your honeymoon and make sure your passports are up to date.

- Book the wedding cars.

- Arrange an appointment for dress fittings for you and your bridesmaids.

- Arrange fittings for the groom and his groomsmen.

- If some of your guests are living abroad, contact them to let them know the date of the wedding.

- Arrange your pre-marriage course.

Four months

- Shop for wedding rings. Bear in mind, if you are having them ordered and/or engraved, it may take six weeks or more before they are ready for collection.

- Meet with the florist and decide on the wedding flowers.

- Decide on wedding favours for the guests.

- Buy the gifts for bridesmaids and groomsmen.

- Book the wedding cake.

- Start compiling the mass booklet.

Three months

- Confirm the booking details with the hotel and church.

- Run through the guest list for a final time.

- Arrange hair and make-up trials.

- If you have a page boy, buy a ring pillow.

- Start considering the music options for your first dance.

Two months

- Buy stamps for the wedding invitations.

- Decide on the outfit you will wear the day after the wedding.

- Post the wedding invitations.

- Meet with the photographer/videographer to discuss ideas or special requests.

- Shop for wedding lingerie.

One month

- Make a list of invitation acceptances and refusals.

- Buy thank you cards to post to guests after the wedding. If you receive gifts in the run-up to the wedding, compose and send thank you notes straight away so that you are not left with an abundance of cards to write after the wedding.

- Give the final guest numbers to the hotel.

- If you are having a tan applied, make your appointment a month in advance.

- Finalise the jewellery you plan to wear.

- Arrange your 'something old, something new, something borrowed, and something blue'.

One week

- Have your bridesmaid arrange your wedding emergency bag.

- Have a wedding rehearsal.

- Confirm appointments with hairstylist and beautician.

- Organise your clothes and toiletries in a suitcase and arrange for one of your family members to bring it to the hotel on the day of the wedding.

- Confirm times with photographer, florist, videographer and the baker delivering the wedding cake.

- Make sure you have a button-down shirt to wear on the morning of the wedding when you are getting your hair and make-up done.

- Most importantly of all, relax!

EMERGENCY BAG

Essentially, your emergency bag is a kit of wedding-day necessities and emergency items to cover the unexpected should anything occur to you or one of the bridal party. Give the list of items you need to your bridesmaids as they are responsible for putting the bag together and bringing it to the hotel on the day itself. The only items you will have to add to the bag on the morning are your make-up (for touch-ups) and your perfume. Don't forget to include the necessary make-up brushes as well.

Items for the bag

Miscellaneous

- Spare safety pins for repairs or in case the florist forgets them for the corsages.

- Masking/sewing tape for broken bouquet handles, falling hems.

- Super glue for fixing shoe heels, loose diamonds in accessories or tiaras.

- Aspirin/headache painkillers.

- Band-aids for blisters.

- Antacid tablets to settle nervous and upset stomachs.

- Any prescription medications the bride or groom may need.

- Drinking straws – these will prevent the bride and bridesmaids ruining their lipstick when taking a drink of water, particularly in between photographs.

- Spare earring backs.

- A list of key people (florist, priest, limo driver, DJ, hotel, photographer) and their phone numbers.

Hair and make-up

- Hair pins.

- Nail polish, and extra fake nails and glue.

- Hairbrush and comb.

- Deodorant.

- Hairspray.

- Moist towelettes and tissues.

- Nail file.

- Cotton wool buds.

Attire

- Buttons should be collected from all the 'spares' that came with the bride's and bridesmaids' dresses.

- Clear nail polish to stop runs in tights.

- Sewing kit (with scissors and thread).

- Dressmakers' chalk or white chalk to cover any stains on the wedding dress.

Louis' Top Tips

- When travelling with a suit, carry it in a suit bag. If packing it in a suitcase, turn it inside out and fold it properly. If the fabric is good, it won't crease that much. When you arrive at your destination, place it on a hanger immediately.

- If you wear glasses, then tone down your tie. Don't go for busy patterns.

- If you want to remove soft creases from a suit, hang it in a bathroom and turn on the shower. The steam generated by the shower should be sufficient to remove the creases.

- A broad man should wear stripes as it will slim his frame. He should also go for elegantly decorative ties.

- A thin man who wants to look broader should wear a dark plain suit and a plain tie.

- It's often said that a short man should not wear a pinstripe garment as it will only make him look shorter but, at the same time, they say a tall man shouldn't wear pinstripe as it will make him look taller. There is no right and wrong when it comes to pinstripe. It's all in the eye of the beholder.

- A man who is small and slim should wear plain clothes; never anything too busy. The understated look is key.

- A man with a beer belly should wear braces with his trousers. It will help to detract from the midriff area.

- If you are wearing a black suit, always wear black socks. In the business world, colourful socks are not acceptable. Stick to dark grey or black.

- If wearing a brown belt, pair it with brown shoes. If wearing a black belt, then wear black shoes. Don't mix brown with black.

- People mess around with 'black tie' suits. They sometimes buy them with stripes or they might buy them in a different colour, like blue, but there's nothing that will beat a nice, plain, black suit with a white shirt and a black tie or bow tie.

You can't change the suit but you can certainly change the accessories!

- You can't reinvent the business suit. It's pretty much the same each season because there's not much else that can be done with it. If men want to embrace the latest trends, then they can do so with the accessories such as ties and shirts. The trends always start in the ladies section. If, for example, purple was the big colour for ladies wear this season, then next season it will be the main colour for menswear. Men shouldn't be afraid of colour. There was a time when men wouldn't dream of wearing pink but, today, you see it everywhere.

- If you can fit two fingers in between the neckline and the cuff, then you should be fine. Sometimes, if the shirt is too tight, it can make the man look extremely uncomfortable whereas if it's too big, it doesn't look right.

- If attending a wedding, show respect to the bride and groom by wearing a tie to the church. It is acceptable to take it off for the reception. If invited to the evening of a wedding, a plain black suit is the appropriate attire.

- Wearing ill-fitting clothes is a big mistake made by a lot men. This is why it's so important to go to the right people and be fitted correctly. If you want to push the boat out, then wear a waistcoat with your suit. Don't wear it all the time, just now and then.

Maternity Style

I have a great passion for life. I'm content, I'm happy, I have fulfilled many of my dreams and dealt with many challenges, but I still regard motherhood as one of my proudest achievements. As any parent will tell you, it's not easy! I have seven years under my belt with my daughter Sophie and five years with my son Dalton.

When I was pregnant with Sophie, I remember craving every food available! As a result, my weight increased and I distinctly remember being just five months pregnant and looking like a woman about to give birth! But, when I was pregnant with Dalton, I devoured grapes and craved olive oil on everything I ate. I was also much fitter and healthier and my figure seemed to return in no time, which was an added bonus!

Following Sophie's birth, I struggled to lose the baby weight. In fact, when I was working in my boutique, a well-meaning customer asked me when I my baby was due, which would have been a perfectly valid question had I not already given birth to Sophie three months earlier!

Ladies don't let your post-natal weight bring you down. Remember, you were nine months gaining the weight, so realistically it's going to take nine months and more to lose it. What's more, you don't need to hide your weight under baggy ill-fitting clothes. With my help, you can easily create a varied wardrobe that flatters your changing shape and serves you with both quality and longevity.

Emma Bunton in her LBMD
- little black maternity dress.

MATERNITY STYLE KNOW-HOW

Being pregnant is difficult enough without having to resign yourself to wearing dark, baggy tops and dungarees. Indeed it's fair to say maternity clothes have had not had the best reputation in the past when it comes to style. Fortunately, ladies, times have changed and maternity wear is now more stylish than ever.

First and foremost, set yourself a budget before you begin shopping and force yourself to stick to it. You will be tempted to splurge but just remember that your bump is constantly changing and certain items may not fit you as comfortably after a few weeks. The key to establishing a diverse and fashionable maternity wardrobe is to invest in a few staple maternity items and build around them with more inexpensive pieces.

Here are a few tips to help you stay stylish and comfortable throughout those nine special months.

Transitional clothes

Your transitional wardrobe is what will carry you through that awkward phase during the second trimester where you begin to outgrow your normal clothes but may still be too small for maternity wear.

Alessandra Ambrosio injects plenty
of colour into her maternity style.

When you reach this stage, begin by buying a few inexpensive staple items such as shirts, long tops, leggings and jeans, in a size bigger than you would normally are. These should discreetly conceal your new bump in a stylish, comfortable way. Even at this stage, comfort should be your priority, so swap your fitted trousers for inconspicuous elasticated waistbands. Begin sourcing maternity clothes the moment your bump begins to show, but don't be tempted to resign your transitional items to the attic too quickly. You will need them in the months following the pregnancy when your body starts to return to its pre-pregnancy size.

Comfort

It goes without saying that comfort is a maternity must but that does not mean you have to sacrifice your style. Forget the myths that suggest comfort cannot be achieved in stylish clothing. In fact, when it comes to maternity wear, stylish comfort can be found in a number of key pieces.

- Try to look for clothes that will stretch as your body grows. Jersey fabric, for example, is a wonderfully flexible fabric that is very soft and comfortable. It's also important to look for fabrics that stretch discreetly. When trying on clothes, ask yourself if it looks as though it is being stretched. Good quality maternity wear fabric should not appear stretched.

- If you don't like the idea of your bump peeping out between your trousers and your top, then invest in a bump band or a long, stretch T-shirt. This will cover any exposed skin.

- In winter, stay warm by layering rather than relying on heavy fabrics. That way, if you suddenly get too hot, you can remove a layer (such as a rib-knit cardigan) rather than having to completely change your outfit.

- Steer clear of clothes that dig into your midriff. They will eventually become more and more uncomfortable. Instead, look out for maternity clothes that have a stylishly disguised elastic waistband.

- Loose sweatpants are wonderful for those off-days where you just want to stay curled up under a duvet. They will also be a necessity for when you are doing your pregnancy exercises. Likewise, a maternity sports bra will provide you with endless comfort when you are out exercising or walking.

- Buy only a few maternity pieces at any one time. Your bump is constantly changing and items that were once the epitome of cosiness will lose their comfort appeal faster than you think.

Denise Van Outen combines pregnancy with style.

- Don't forget to check the lining of your maternity clothes when you are trying them on. The fabric should not irritate or itch your skin in any way.

- Most shops will have a prosthetic tummy that you can try on when checking the fit of your maternity clothes. Needless to say, it is not 100 per cent accurate as everyone's bump is different but it will give you an idea of how the clothes will look with a bigger bump. Your bump will change in many different ways as your pregnancy progresses, so don't rely too heavily on the prosthetic bump when trying on clothes. It's usually best to wait until the latter stages of your second trimester before buying clothes for your third trimester.

- Maternity clothes can be expensive so shop around and be creative. If, for example, you have a very large bump, browse the plus-size section of department stores for casual wear. Don't forget to also have a look in the menswear section of department stores for extra large stylish T-shirts and plain shirts.

- If you plan to breast feed, look out for nursing tops and dresses. Nursing sleepwear likewise will also come in handy for those quick night feeds.

Maternity bra

Q. Why do I need to buy a maternity bra? Can I not just wear my regular bra but in a bigger size?

A. Maternity bras, unlike normal bras, are specifically designed to accommodate the drastic changes your breasts will undergo during and after pregnancy. They provide a significant amount of extra support for the breasts as they become larger and more sensitive. The hook closures at the back of maternity bras are also designed to coincide with the stages of your pregnancy. The first hook (i.e. the tightest hook) is usually used during the early stages of pregnancy while the last hook (i.e the loosest) is used during the final stages. Even if you buy your normal bra in a larger size, it will not provide the adequate comfort and support your bust needs during pregnancy.

Q. At what stage of the pregnancy do I buy a maternity bra?

A. Women will usually require a maternity bra by the fourth month of pregnancy, however it's perfectly fine to begin wearing one in the earlier stages. The general rule of thumb is that you should start wearing a maternity bra when your breasts have begun to swell and become more tender.

Q. I will soon be shopping for a maternity bra and was wondering if there were any specific features I should look out for?

A. If you find yourself getting hot easily, then look for a maternity bra that is made from 100 per cent cotton. A comfortable maternity bra should have wide cushioned shoulder straps to support your growing bust. The bra's band should lie on the ribcage and should at no point rise up onto the breast tissue. As you will be wearing your maternity bras for many months before and after your baby is born, make sure you buy good-quality maternity bras that have three or more back closures so as to allow you to adjust the bra in conjunction with your changing bust size.

Maternity work style

When it comes to dressing around your bump for work, the key is to keep your look tailored and classically simple. Look for versatile maternity items that you can dress up or down. Such items would include black and grey trousers, black wrap dress, pencil skirt with front panels for your bump, A-line skirt, white and black shirts, cardigans, blazer and long black/white tank tops. When you have the basics, you should be able to recreate many different looks by mixing and matching (not to mention accessorising) the various items.

Here are some tips to help you achieve a polished professional look.

- Black trousers (with front panels for support) as well as a good-quality shirt that fits loosely around the bump are the two staple items of any maternity work wardrobe and will see you through any occasion.

- During the earlier stages of your pregnancy, see if you can mix your usual work wear with your transitional clothes.

- Plain A-line skirts and dresses offer a very elegant professional look particularly when paired with a tailored shirt or top.

- Three-quarter-length sleeves and shawls are fantastic for hiding any extra weight you may gain on your upper arms.

- A flattering neckline is pivotal. Scoop necks and V-necks are ideal as long as they are not too low or revealing.

- Footwear for the office should have a small heel, no more than two inches.

Halle Be

- Office air-conditioning is unpredictable at the best of times, so avoid those unexpected hot flashes by wearing layered clothing, such as a long tank top underneath a cardigan.

- When shopping for tops, buy them slightly longer than what you would normally go for. You will need the extra length for coverage when your bump means the top will rise up slightly.

- It's a good idea to limit your work wear to strong solid colours, however if you want to inject a dash of colour, turn to your accessories. Anything from an elegant broach to a neck scarf can instantly brighten up your outfit without detracting from your professional appearance in any way.

- Tops or jackets with shoulder pads are ideal for balancing out your shape. For a particularly sharp look, pair it with a pencil skirt or black trousers.

- Wrap cardigans are so stylish and comfortable, and are ideal for the workplace.

- If your job involves sitting at a desk for hours on end, then avoid trousers where the waistband even slightly rubs your stomach.

Colour

Try to inject your look with colour whenever possible. Accessories such as handbags and jewellery are particularly good for introducing a dash of instant colour into your look. Whether it's a red belt, a purple scarf or a turquoise necklace, it will make such a difference to your style and your mood! If you tend to dress mostly in black, then make a point of giving yourself a colour boost particularly during those days when you're feeling tired. I always advise women not to limit their wardrobes to black and navy shades. Instead show off your beautiful bump in tops that are bright and feminine.

MATERNITY MUST HAVES

Jeans, trousers and khakis

A pair of good-quality maternity trousers is a must have in every pregnancy wardrobe. Black maternity trousers are particularly good for dressing up, while maternity jeans, khakis and leggings are wonderful for comfortable everyday wear. It is definitely a good idea to spend a little extra for quality maternity trousers as you will be wearing them so often throughout your pregnancy as well as in the months following the birth.

Sometimes, women are often tempted to skip the expense of maternity trousers by buying ordinary trousers in a bigger size, but this is not advisable. As your bump grows, these trousers will become uncomfortable very quickly. Ordinary trousers, regardless of their size, are not designed to accommodate a bump, nor are they made with the needs of a pregnant woman in mind. Maternity trousers on the other hand, have a number of specific features such as breathable fabric and a discreet, elasticated waistband, that will make your life more comfortable!

You will find that some maternity trousers are designed to sit under the bump while others will sit over the bump. Maternity trousers that sit directly on the bump are less popular as they cannot be used in the months following the birth.

The key to finding long-lasting maternity trousers is to look for durable fabric and stretchable front/side panels that will expand with your bump. A flattering cut is also very important. Bootleg is not only one of the most stylish cuts, it will also help balance out your overall shape. As always, the only way to find out which cut will best suit your shape is to visit a maternity shop and try them all on. If, like some women, you hate the feel of an elasticated waistband then look for drawstring trousers. If you are particularly short or tall and can't find maternity trousers to fit try shopping online. Know your exact measurements before you buy and don't forget to allow an extra inch or two for comfort.

A-line tops and shirts

Baggy tops are neither classy or feminine, so when adding to the staple items of your maternity wardrobe, try to go for long, stylish, A-line tops. These will appear fitted on top but will flow out to allow enough space for your growing bump. Empire waist tops are also very pretty when worn by expectant mothers. Your bust will more than likely need all the extra support it can get, so it may be a good idea to resign the strapless items to the back of your wardrobe. When shopping for tops during the earlier stages of your pregnancy, always make sure there is enough growing room in the bust area.

Wrap dress, dresses and skirts

A wrap dress is a maternity must have. It is elegant, stylish, extremely comfortable and better still, it can be worn to any occasion! If you buy a black wrap dress, don't forget to inject it with some colour through jewellery, shoes, a handbag, broach or a neck scarf.

When buying skirts and dresses during the early stages of pregnancy, avoid hemlines that sit above the knee at all costs. The more your bump grows,

the higher the hemline will rise up. Most maternity skirts and dresses on the other hand will have elasticated front panels that stretch along with your bump.

A-line skirts and dresses are definitely one of the most flattering and elegant styles for pregnant women.

If you are quite tall, maxi dresses are a fantastic option particularly if your hormones are playing up and you're left suddenly feeling quite hot regardless of the season. Naturally, maxi dresses are most appropriate for those summer months when the heat can leave you feeling quite clammy. Should the weather turn cold, however, pair your dress with a shawl or a cardigan. Steer clear of halter-neck dresses as these will not provide adequate support for your breasts. Instead opt for dresses with wide straps and breathable fabric.

Shoes

If you find yourself lamenting the days when you could wear your trendy high heels with ease, you will be pleased to know that pregnancy does not mean having to sacrifice stylish footwear. There is an amazing array of inexpensive pumps and low wedges available in a variety of styles, patterns and colours.

Look for shoes that will not restrict your feet. Elasticated pumps and gladiator sandals for instance are particularly comfortable. When shopping for 'maternity shoes', look for ones that have good arch support, non-slippery soles and, preferably, a cushioned lining for extra relief for tired feet. If you find that your shoes are somewhat uncomfortable, bring them to a cobbler and see if they can adjusted in any way.

Don't risk wearing heels when pregnant. For a start, your feet will suffer immensely. Secondly, your new bump may have slightly disturbed your balance and wearing heels will only increase your risk of serious injury should you become unsteady.

Trust me, slip-on shoes will become your new best friend when your bump starts preventing you from bending over to tie your laces.

Nightwear

Proper nightwear is important for a restful night's sleep. Look out for maternity pyjamas that are made from breathable fabrics such as jersey cotton. If you need extra support, look out for nightwear that has built in support cups/panels.

Tina Leonard

Consumer Rights

Consumer Rights

ASK THE EXPERT... TINA LEONARD

"It doesn't matter how much or little money is involved, it's the principle of the matter. You have rights so claim them."

Tina Leonard

We always associate consumer rights with shopping, but have you ever stopped to think about your rights as a consumer when you avail of services from places such as a hair salon or dry cleaner? Do you know your specific rights as an online consumer?

When I spoke with established consumer rights consultant Tina Leonard, I was absolutely amazed by amount of information regarding consumer rights that so many of us are not familiar with. I have always maintained that knowledge is power. Tina's advice is testament to this.

Dry Cleaning

When you drop your clothes in to the dry cleaner you are basically paying for a service and, according to the Sale of Goods and Supply of Services Act 1980, a service should be carried out with necessary skill, care and diligence and any parts used should be of merchantable quality.

So, those signs that you sometimes see in a dry cleaner, the ones that say something like "We are not responsible for buttons falling off or zips breaking", are not only incorrect they are also against the law!

In fact, if your button falls off or if the item being cleaned is damaged, then it is the dry cleaner's responsibility to remedy the situation. If they cannot provide a repair then a reimbursement for the cost of the item may be in order.

If you are looking for a reimbursement for something, whether it was damaged and cannot be repaired, or whether the dry cleaner has lost it, you should get proof of the cost of the item.

Look through old credit card or debit card statements to find proof of the cost, or go back to the shop where you bought it and ask them to write the cost of the item on headed paper. Of course, if that item is still on sale you're in luck. If not, then hopefully a good retailer will be able to help you out.

But remember don't be greedy! If the dress is two years old you can't expect reimbursement for the full price you paid, after all you've had several wears already!

If the item of clothing you are handing in to the dry cleaner is delicate, you may be asked to sign a form waiving the responsibility of the dry cleaner in the case of something going wrong. Guess what? That means what it says – if they damage the item they may not be responsible. Think carefully before signing anything or better still go to a dry cleaner that can carry out the service with confidence and responsibility.

Hair/Beauty salons

Remember that when you're getting your hair done or a pampering treatment at a beauty salon, you are still buying a service and you have rights.

Under the Sale of Goods and Supply of Services Act 1980, the service must be carried out with the necessary skill and due care and diligence.

This means that if something goes wrong you have redress and can expect a repair, replacement or refund.

When it comes to hairdressing salons, there is a statutory order that obliges them to display their prices. This should make it easier for you to choose where you want to go, based on the prices charged. Usually, different prices are charged depending on the experience of the various hairdressers. So if the price display indicates that a hair cut is from a certain price, don't be shy in asking exactly what you can expect to pay, in order to avoid 'bill shock' later on.

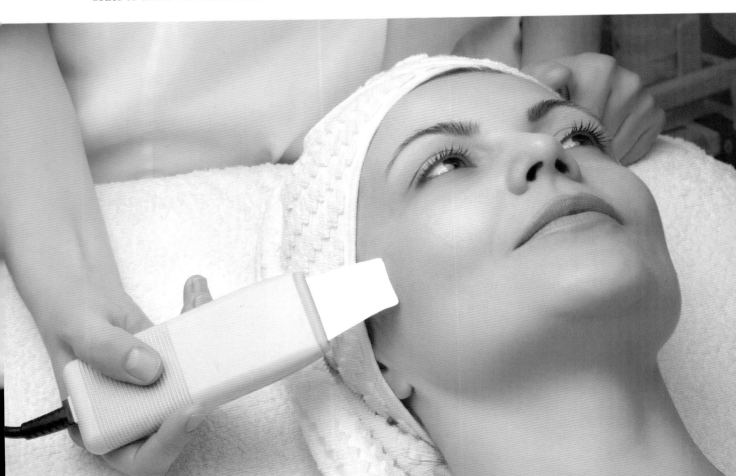

It is somewhat difficult to offer points of advice in relation to your rights if you don't like the haircut or colour you have been given.

As I stated above, the Sale of Goods and Supply of Services Act 1980 states that the service has to be carried out with the necessary skill, due care and diligence and that any parts used must be of merchantable quality. If, however, you requested a certain style and the style you ended up with was a bit different and you hated it, it would be difficult to argue that the hairdresser didn't have the required skill or didn't take enough care. What about your expectations of how a style might look on you? What conversation did you have with the stylist about what you wanted before she or he went in with the scissors?

The same applies with hair colour. If you have requested honey blonde and ended up a shade of chestnut, then there is clearly a problem and a remedy should be given. But just because the colour isn't how you imagined it would be doesn't necessarily mean the dye was faulty, applied incorrectly or that a different colour was used to the one requested.

Having said that, there could be a breach of contract if your scalp or hair is burned or damaged, or if, let's say, the stylist was so incompetent you are left half bald!

They are extreme examples, but in any case the best practice is to try to negate the possibility of anything going wrong in the first place. If you are going to a new stylist find out how experienced she or he is; talk things through carefully about what you want and ask whether what you want is possible for you (after all one style can look completely different on two different heads of hair). Discuss how a particular hair colour is likely to look on your crowning glory and whether the shade shown on the colour chart is likely to be slightly different when on your hair.

Shopping online

More and more of us are discovering bargains online. For instance, there are some great sites for sourcing clothes, but what if the fabulous frock doesn't fit you when it arrives and you finally get a chance to try it on?

Rest assured that when you buy online you actually have more rights than when you buy on the high street.

The same rules apply to faulty products or ones that are not 'as described' in that you are entitled to a repair, replacement or refund from the seller.

In addition, under the Distance Selling Directive, when you buy online you are entitled to a cooling-off period of seven days from the day of delivery. During those seven days, you can inform the seller that you don't want to keep the item and are going to send it back – and you don't even have to give a reason! This rule doesn't cover perishables, flights or accommodation, CDs and DVDs that have the seal removed or for goods that are personalised or made to order. But the cooling-off period is very handy for clothes, shoes, accessories and more, so don't be afraid to use it.

Do bear in mind, though, that you may have to pay for return postage costs when sending something back because you don't like it. However, you do not have to pay for the return postage costs if you are returning something because it is faulty or not the size you asked for.

By the way, these rules cover you for shopping all over the European Union, so you can shop safely even when you look for bargains farther afield.

Always be careful about which websites you buy from. Make sure you have the full contact details, including a postal address and telephone number, of the web trader you plan to do business with. Otherwise, how will you contact them if something goes wrong? If you are thinking of shopping on a site you've never heard of, why not carry out an internet search on the web trader – you'll soon find any negative reports.

FAULTY GOODS

When you buy something, whether it's a dress or a washing machine, it is supposed to be fit for its purpose and 'as described' – in other words it should do what it says on the tin.

If not then, under the Sale of Goods and Supply of Services Act 1980, you are entitled to a repair, replacement or refund and the obligation to provide a remedy lies with the shop in which you made the purchase.

Let's say you wear a new pair of shoes twice and the heel falls off, or your new pair of trousers shrinks to nothing in the wash, even though you followed the care instructions. If the shoes are faulty or if those care instructions were incorrect, then you should expect a remedy.

When something goes wrong with a brand-new item, you should expect a replacement or refund straight away. If the item is older, you should expect a repair first. The retailer can opt to have the item tested to see if it is faulty. If they say it is not faulty but you disagree put your complaint in writing to them.

If this doesn't work then you can make an application to the Small Claims Court. This will cost you a non-refundable fee of €15 and you can claim up to €2,000. Check out www.courts.ie for further information on the Small Claims Court procedure.

Your consumer rights only come into play if the item you buy turns out to be faulty or not as described. These rights do not entitle you to bring something back just because you don't like it or it doesn't fit. This is up to the shop itself so always check their returns policy. While you're at it, always try on clothing on before you buy. You don't want to find yourself stuck with a top that doesn't fit from a shop that does not allow returns on unwanted items.

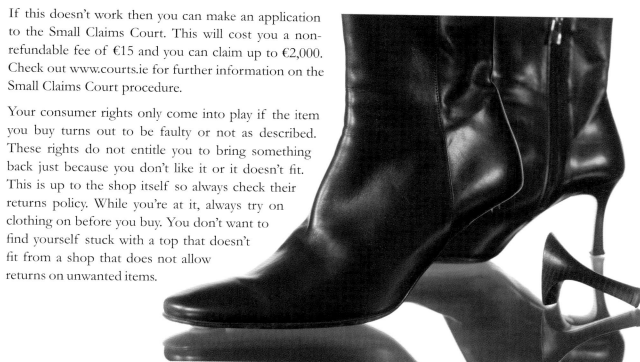

SALES

We're all tempted when we see a sale sign and you can rest assured that your consumer rights are exactly the same in a sale as when you buy at full price.

It's also worth bearing in mind that when something is shown with a sale price or with a 'percentage off' sign, the original price should be displayed. The original price should have been used for a 'reasonable period' prior to the sale. This is recommended as twenty-eight days, or fourteen days for perishables or seasonal products.

We all know that, during a sale, old stock may be brought out from storage and it is unlikely that old stock was on sale for twenty-eight days within the previous three months. That's not a problem as long as those items are described as "old stock". After all, you need to know what you're buying.

Always remember to thoroughly check the item before you buy.

During sales your rights are the same, but the shop's own returns policy, which is separate to your rights and entirely up to the shop, may change. For example, instead of offering twenty-eight days to return unwanted items, the shop might only provide ten days during a sale. Always ask to avoid disappointment later.

WARRANTIES

There is a lot of confusion out there about what you can claim under a manufacturer's warranty against what rights you have under consumer law.

The first thing you should know is that the two are entirely separate.

A warranty, or guarantee, from the seller or manufacturer is a contract between you and them and is in addition to your rights.

Your statutory rights cannot be taken away from you – even if you don't have any warranty, or if your warranty has expired, you still have your rights.

Each warranty will be different and can be useful if, for example, the shop where you bought the item has closed down, or if the warranty offers more than your consumer rights, such as accidental damage.

Here are some things to check in the warranty:

- How long is it valid for?

- Does it cover call-out charges as well as repairs?

- Does it place a limit on the number or repairs or start charging after a number of repairs?

- Does it cover replacement?

- Does it cover accidental damage?

- If you buy in another jurisdiction is cover limited to that country?

- Do you have to register to activate the guarantee?

Very often when you go back to a store with a faulty electrical item, they will refer you back to the manufactuer and your warranty. That's fine if the terms of your warranty will cover the problem, but what if they don't or if your warranty has expired? The retailer (and not the manufacturer) is legally obliged to provide a remedy for a faulty product or one that turns out to be not 'as described'. So don't let them fob you off!

Style Clinic

Q. I love crisp, fluid styles like those worn by Victoria Beckham but how can I adapt these styles for the workplace?

A. Victoria Beckham may be high fashion but her style can easily be recreated with high street offerings and adapted to suit the workplace. In fact, quite a lot of Victoria's style can be copied using classic pieces, such as white/ black shirt, black dress or grey trousers/skirt. Below are some looks that you can recreate using those classics.

Q. My legs are my best asset, however I sometimes worry that my skirts are too short. What is the acceptable length for a mini skirt worn by a woman in her early thirties?

A. The most flattering hemline is the one that sits right at the knee. When it comes to determining whether or not your skirt/dress hemline is too short, all you have to do is bend over slightly. If your underwear is visible, then your hemline is too short.

Q. I'm sure you have been asked this question time and time again, but can you give me some advice on dressing for a job interview? I want to stand out but look professional at the same time.

A. You can boast an impressive CV and possess the most amazing charisma, but if you walk into an interview wearing the wrong attire, you will pretty much destroy your chances of impressing the interviewer.

First impressions are crucial so don't assume your CV will do all the talking.

Remember, your prospective employer will be taking all aspects of your appearance into consideration. When you are answering questions, your interviewer will be observing details such as the condition of your nails and hair. An interviewee with dirty unpolished nails would suggest that they pay little attention to the smaller details. In your interviewer's eyes, a neat appearance indicates a neat, organised worker. Wearing a watch is also crucial as it signifies punctuality in a person.

In terms of interview fashion, it's important that you familiarise yourself with the company and their dress code. For instance, if you are being interviewed for a position with a trendy retail company then your interviewer will be looking for someone with a natural taste for chic, edgy style. Some companies prefer their employees to wear suits and smart professional attire whereas others like their staff to show off their creative style. Research the company dress code and then adjust your outfit accordingly.

One thing that is certain however is that jeans and anything with sequins are never acceptable for a job interview.

If, following your research, you are still unsure, play it safe by wearing a tailored dress or suit. I think it goes without saying that you need to make sure everything is clean and crease-free! To inject an element of individuality, just accessorise. Elegant items such as a neck scarf or a broach are very appropriate.

Keep jewellery to a minimum and avoid bracelets and bangles that jingle when you move your hand. Simple pearl earrings and a watch will work fine. Make sure your nails are filed, buffed and polished. No strong colours, just a light manicure will suffice.

Don't fold your CV and store it in your handbag. Instead bring a separate folder for holding whatever documents your interviewer may require. You will look far more professional and organised. If stress makes you sweat, then be prepared by bringing along compact powder, deodorant and dry shampoo. Above all, believe in yourself and walk into your interview with confidence, a good attitude and a smile.

Top Tip

Ask yourself what your interviewer will be expecting. If for example you are being interviewed for a position in an industry like fashion or entertainment, your interviewer will be expecting you to wear chic, stylish attire.

Actress Emma Thompson uses make-up and not surgery to emphasise her features.

Q. I'm getting older, but I don't want to look old! Cosmetic surgery is not something I am interested in. Any advice on how I can defy the years?

A. The right make-up can take years off your appearance. To find out which shades you should be using, book an appointment (or a make-up lesson) with a make-up artist. When they are finished, you will see just how the right shade of foundation and blusher can give you a more youthful appearance. There are so many tips that you can learn to your benefit. It's just a matter of asking the experts. In fact, something as simple as having your eyebrows shaped and groomed can give you the effects of an eyelift. Don't forget to ask the make-up artist to write out a list of the various products and brushes they have used.

Hair is also an important factor when it comes to reducing your appearance-age. The wrong style can add years to your face whereas the right style can make you look refreshed and younger. Visit a wig shop to try out different styles of cuts and colours. If you're still very unsure about what kind of style will work for you, book a consultation with an established hairstylist. They will know exactly what you should go for.

Take an honest look at your wardrobe. Can you picture Catherine Deneuve or Elle MacPherson wearing the items you see in front of you? As you get older, you need to look more towards tailored classics. These include, cashmere sweaters, a good quality white shirt, black trousers, a blazer or a twin-set paired with a pencil skirt.

Dump the dowdy clothes and embrace colour. Look at your outfit and ask yourself where it can be improved? Would a chiffon scarf make a difference? How about a trendier handbag? Or perhaps a large chic belt? Accessories and jewellery can easily be used to help reduce your appearance-age.

"In France, women are allowed to have really big bags under their eyes like mine and they're allowed to get older and still be female, beautiful and sexy. But in America everybody wants you to be size zero and I don't like it."

Emma Thompson

Q. My handbag is quite heavy and I am quite concerned that it may lead to neck and back pain. How can I be sure it won't?

A. You're absolutely right to be concerned. We tend to carry our lives in our handbags. From magazines and bottles of water to umbrellas and heavy make-up bags, it all adds up in terms of weight. Here are a few tips to help you keep your handbag from causing you pain.

- Weigh your handbag on the bathroom scales, first with the contents and then without. By doing this, you will know exactly what weight you are carrying on your shoulders.

- If we're being honest with ourselves, a lot of what we carry in our handbags is clutter. This is why it's crucial to make a point of de-cluttering your bag every night. This also includes clearing out your purse of small change.

- When you are planning your day ahead, think about what you will need to bring with you and ask yourself if there are any items that can be left in the car.

- Pack only the essential items in your make-up bag rather than bringing everything along. For instance, rather than packing a foundation bottle, buy a small travel tub and pour some foundation into it.

- When carrying your bag, change shoulders often and leave it down whenever you can. Try if you can to choose a bag with wide straps as these will help distribute the weight over a broader area of your shoulder.

Q. I want to get a suit made but have no idea what style to go for. Where should I look to for ideas?

A. Go for a classic style but don't be afraid to look to the fashion pages for inspiration. This will help you decide what kind of styles and features you like. Remember, a suit doesn't have to mean 'trouser suit', you can go for a skirt suit if you want to look sharp yet feminine.

You can never go wrong with a black or navy suit, but there's no harm to look at various other colours that may flatter your skin tone. If you want to go for a dark suit, look at pinstripe fabric and see if it suits you.

Next, you need to think about the fabric and what you will require from the one you choose for your suit. Are you looking for a fabric that is breathable or are you looking for material that will keep you warm? Will you be travelling a lot with your suit? If so, then you will need a fabric that won't crease easily. Your tailor will be able to address any concerns or questions you may have, but it's still a good idea to research and establish what you like and don't like.

1. Diane Von Furstenberg
2. Eva Longoria

Q. I find that my nail polish tends to chip after a day's wear. How can I make it last longer. I hate having to reapply it almost every night.

A. When it comes to nail care, women would be better off not wearing nail polish at all than to wear it chipped. Fortunately, there are ways of preventing those unsightly cracks from appearing too soon. To increase the longevity of your nail colour, you need to buy good-quality polish. They may be slightly more expensive, but the resulting finish will look much better and will last longer. OPI is a fantastic brand used by many models and celebrities.

Top Tip

Castor oil is wonderful for curing dry and brittle nails. By massaging the nails with the oil, you are injecting them with a kick of moisture. If you do this every day and you should notice your nails looking healthy and shiny within weeks.

- Before you even open the lid of the polish bottle, you need to prepare your nails. After washing and filing your nails, dip your fingers in some white vinegar. This will remove all traces of natural oils thereby making it easier for the polish to stick to the nail for longer.

- When you go to apply the nail colour, do so with just three strokes. One for the middle, followed by two more for either side.

- When the colour has set, apply a top coat using a good-quality polish. This will help seal the colour in place and will also act as a barrier against anything that may chip your varnish.

- Your polish will not be fully dry for at least an hour. To speed up the drying process dip your nails into a basin filled with ice-cold water for thirty seconds. Only do this after you have given your nails twenty minutes of air drying.

- Apply one swipe of top coat polish every morning. This will help strengthen the protective barrier against chipping.

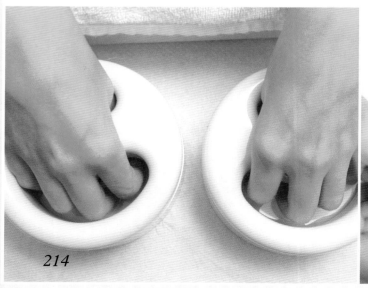

Q. There are so many mornings when I don't have time to style my hair. Could you recommend any quick hairstyles? I'm tired of relying on the ponytail!

A. Tousled

The tousled, just-out-of-bed look is very popular and can look amazing when done right. Tie your hair into a high bun before you go to bed. The following morning, you will have a beautiful wave running through your hair. To define the wave a bit more, take a large-barrelled curling iron or a GHD straightener and curl some of the strands. If you want to keep your hair off your face, then secure it into a messy bun. This is a look sported by many celebrities at formal events.

Braid hair band

Look out for accessories that will give you a polished look in little time. One such accessory is the braid hair band (also known as the Alice Band Plait and the Heidi Plait).

These can be found in a variety of shades to suit the different hair colours so it's just a matter of finding the one that best suits you. To give your hair volume before you wear the hair band, apply some dry shampoo to the roots followed by a slick of hairspray. Now slide on the braid hair band. The best thing about this accessory is that it looks good regardless of whether you wear your hair up or down.

Messy side bun

Work some dry shampoo or styling cream into the roots to give the hair texture. Next flip your head upside down, and gather your hair. Flip your head back up and tightly secure the messy bun at the side of your head with a hair tie. Forget using serum. This look works best when there are plenty of fly-away strands.

1. Jessica Biel
2. Sienna Miller
3. Mischa Barton

Q. This might sound like a silly question, but when it comes to SPF, I am clueless. For instance, if I apply it in the morning, will that suffice for the entire day? If I am wearing a fake tan as well as make-up, do I even need to wear SPF? Could you give me some general advice on finding the right SPF for me?

A. Don't assume that a higher SPF means longer coverage. Regardless of the strength of your SPF, you still have to reapply throughout the day particularly if the weather is quite hot.

- You should get into the habit of applying your SPF in the morning, even on cloudy days. Remember, just because you can't see the sun doesn't mean those sun rays are not still seeping through the clouds.

- Sometimes people apply an SPF 20 on top of an SPF 30 and assume they have the combined protection of an SPF 50. This is not the case. If you want an SPF 50, then buy an SPF 50. Don't mix and match.

- Don't forget to apply SPF to your lips, ears, hands and feet. These are all too often overlooked. Always carry a sunscreen lip balm so that you can reapply the SPF to your lips on a regular basis.

- Foundation and powder will provide some protection from the sun but not to the extend that SPF will protect. A lot of cosmetics contain sunscreen, but this isn't always adequate. You still need to apply your SPF before you apply your make-up. Rather than using a separate moisturiser and SPF, use a sunscreen that doubles up as a moisturiser instead.

Q. How can I wear cropped jeans without looking too casual?

A. High heels! Cropped jeans provide the perfect opportunity to show off your fanciest footwear. Wedges also work brilliantly for that casual, chic style.

Don't forget to look towards your accessories when dressing up cropped jeans. A decorative belt or scarf can easily inject some glamour into your look. Just remember the golden rule of style, choose one statement item and keep everything else simple.

Q. I find it so difficult to throw out clothes because I keep thinking, I might wear it some day. Ironically, I feel as though I have nothing to wear! I'm quickly running out of wardrobe space!

A. When women feel they have nothing to wear, their first response is usually to hit the shops and buy. I always advise women to go through their wardrobe and see which items they can update. Take an item and ask yourself why you haven't worn it in some time? Would you wear it more if you dyed it a different colour, changed the buttons or had it shortened? Look at the other items in your wardrobe and see which ones it can be paired with. There are so many potential new looks in your wardrobe, it's just a matter of taking the time and imagination to uncover them. If you haven't worn an item in well over a year, either take it to a charity shop or sell it in a swop shop or on eBay. There are plenty of handbag exchange companies online where you can sell off handbags you no longer use. Don't buy spontaneously. Instead, look at your wardrobe and ask yourself what you need.

Q. I would love to wear red lipstick but I just don't feel confident enough to carry off such a loud colour. I'm so afraid I will look silly. Could you give me any tips for working the red-lipstick look?

A. As I mentioned in the make-up chapter earlier, if you're not one for wearing bright lip colours, it's advisable to try red lipstick at home first. You will more than likely loathe it, but this is only because you're not used to seeing yourself wearing such a bright colour. Don't wipe it off. Instead, leave the lipstick on for an hour and look in the mirror every so often during that hour so as to gradually train your eye to the new look. When the hour is up, you will instinctively know whether or not the red lip shade suits you. Red lipstick tends to bleed, so ensure that you lightly powder your lips with loose face powder before applying lip liner.

- More often than not, when celebrities wear red lipstick, the colour they're wearing is a blend of reds. On that note, don't discard lipsticks you bought on the spur of the moment but haven't worn. Instead, use a lip brush to mix the colour on your lips with other shades.

Hayden Panettiere

lip. This is just the right amount to reflect the light, which in turn will give the appearance of fuller lips.

Q. I want to invest in a coat that will last years and will defy trends. What should I look for?

A. Some of my favourite coats are almost ten years old and I know it will be another ten years before I part with them. The main points to keeping mind when buying a coat that will last is to look for a simple style and good-quality fabric. The less detail in terms of patterns and embroidery, the longer it will last. Strong colours like black, grey, white and camel are timeless. Likewise, trench coats, particularly white, beige and black, never date.

- Usually, those with thin lips shouldn't wear red or dark lipsticks as their lips will only appear smaller. However, this can vary between individuals.

- To keep red lipstick off your teeth, place your index finger in your mouth and close your lips around it. When you pull your finger out, it removes any excess lipstick, thereby preventing it from ending up on your teeth.

- When applying eye or lip make-up, remember the one-or-the-other rule. Don't go heavy on the eyes if you're planning on wearing red or dark lipstick. Likewise, if you're going heavy on the eye make-up, go light on the lips.

- For a matte look, blot the red lipstick by placing a folded ply of tissue paper in between the lips and pressing them together. If on the other hand, you want an injection of glossy shine, apply a slick of Vaseline or clear lip gloss to the centre of the bottom

Angelina Jolie and Fergie embrace
the beauty of simple timeless coats.

Q. I'm in my late thirties and was wondering if I could get away with wearing Ugg boots or if they are really only seen as footwear exclusive to teenagers?

A. I personally don't like the look of Uggs but I think they are wonderful from a comfort perspective, particularly for those early morning school runs. Some people love them; some hate them. I agree they are far from stylish, but they do come in handy when you're standing in a school yard on a freezing winter's morning.

Q. I wear the same style day in, day out and feel as though I'm stuck in a rut. My husband and I don't socialise much so I never have an opportunity to dress up. What can I do?

A. If you dress casual all week, then make a point of dressing up at the weekend. Even if you are only staying in with your partner and enjoying a takeaway and a bottle of wine, make the effort and dress up. Light a candle, set the table and create an atmosphere. You will feel so much better as a result.

Life doesn't have to be mundane; even the most ordinary of situations can be jazzed up! Casual wear can also be sexy if you think outside the box. Look to the high street for nice tops and trousers. Even a plain white cotton top can look chic when you pair it with nice jewellery. Break away from wearing casual clothes and aim for casual-chic! When you invest the effort in your appearance, you will feel much better about yourself and far more confident.

Q. I want to be prepared for every eventuality in my workplace but I hate trying to fit my full make-up bag into my handbag. What items should I bring that will help me be prepared for business meetings and unexpected meetings?

A. Everyone should have a toilet bag in their drawer at work. This should contain a toothbrush, toothpaste, breath mints, hand cream, lip balm, hair brush, travel-size hairspray and hair ties. It's always a good idea to collect those free make-up samples from magazines and shops (provided they are a shade suitable for your skin tone.) and store them in your work toiletries bag. If you want to be extra organised, keep a shawl in your drawer. If you're anything like me, you will spill coffee on your white shirt an hour before an important meeting, so it's a good idea to keep a shawl handy for those emergency moments!

Q. As a mother, I feel so guilty whenever I find myself wanting a day off where I can just do nothing. Do other mothers feel like this?

A. We all have days where we want to stay in our pyjamas and turn a blind eye to the make-up bag. Enjoy those days! Sometimes life can get so hectic between work and kids that it's important to take a day here and there where you can just relax, unwind and do the things that you want to do. It's OK to have an off day! Just get back on track the following day.

DESIGNER RICHARD LEWIS

Dublin's South Frederick Street. Considering this street has been home to great couturists such as Irene Gilbert and Nellie Mulcahy, I think it's fair to say there could never be a more fitting address for the studio of acclaimed designer, Richard Lewis.

When I arrived at Richard's studio for our interview, both he and his team were hard at work, busy preparing for the previewing of his autumn/winter collection which was scheduled to take place in three days. It has to be said that there is something distinctly wonderful about Richard's passion for his craft; a passion that is primarily evident from the fact that even after all these years in the business, and not forgetting the countless accolades he has picked up along the way, the prospect of displaying his new collection to an audience still has the ability to make him somewhat nervous.

One look at the quality of Richard's work and it comes as no surprise to discover that his creations are considered treasured heirlooms in some families, passed down from mother to daughter. Remarkably,

2010 marks forty-five years since Richard graduated from the Grafton Academy of Dress Design and set up his own fashion business, a business that quickly set him well apart from his fellow designers. In 1977, he opened his studio in Dublin's South Frederick Street and has built a steady client base ever since. Even though he is best known for his classic evening wear, he manages to inject a sense of graceful elegance into any garment he turns his hand to.

Richard holds many achievements to his name, most notably the prestigious Satzenbrau Fashion Oscar for Best Spring Collection and a Satzenbrau Special Award, received in 1991, for his outstanding contribution to the fashion industry. The true reflection of his work, however, does not lie in his awards but in his client list, which ranges from women in their twenties to women who have been with him since he opened his studio.

He shared with me his thoughts on fashion and offered his own ten commandments on style!

Q. Richard, what tips would you offer to a woman who is looking to invest in good-quality clothes that will remain timeless and trend-resistant for years to come?

A. Do not buy anything with patterns or prints. Choose solid colours, ones that suit your skin tone. It's important to know what suits you and to trust your own sense of style.

I believe that when it comes to fashion, we should look at the century and not the year. Just because something is in fashion this year doesn't mean you have to wear it. After all, you don't want to end up losing your own

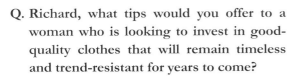

individual sense of style. Be aware of what's in fashion but then choose the items that suit you. Lastly, style should be about the woman looking good in the dress, not the dress looking good on the woman. For instance, if Mary walks into a room wearing one of my dresses and someone remarks on how wonderful she looks, then that's brilliant. If on the other hand, the person remarks that Mary is wearing a Richard Lewis dress, then I have failed. The woman should come first, not the dress.

Q. How important is the correct underwear when it comes to evening wear?

A. I'm a great believer in women wearing the right foundation garments like Spanx shape wear for instance. They give you a very smooth silhouette which is really important when you are wearing an evening gown made from a fabric that skims your body.

Q. What is the best way to eliminate those dreaded creases from an evening gown?

A. For jersey fabric, the best method is to hang it in the bathroom, turn on the shower and allow the steam to get rid of the creases. Another option is to wear the dress and have someone use a hairdryer on the creases!

Q. Your designs are very simplistic, elegant and feminine. In fact, there is something very Parisian about your couture. I could easily imagine them being worn by beautiful French women!

A. The French do style quite well, but the Italians do it better. To be honest, I find the French

style slightly boring whereas the Italians are somewhat edgier and quirkier. I think it's nice to have an edge somewhere in your style.

Q. In your opinion, which one item or accessory can add that touch of sophistication to a woman's overall look?

A. I think the best accessory that works for everyone is a bright smile.

Q. I love that your creations are so timeless. However, do you get fed up of women approaching you and telling you that they still have a dress that they bought from you years ago?

A. I never get fed up of that! I love hearing from them. I spoke with a woman who had bought a dress from me around fifteen years ago. She has worn it many times since then and has now passed it on to her daughter. She said the dress was like part of the family!

Richard Lewis' ten commandments

1. Let your head look to fashion but your heart look to style.
2. Always wear the dress, never let the dress wear you.
3. A dress should hang on your back, not in a wardrobe.
4. What you wear inside can be more important than what you wear outside.
5. Check once in a full length mirror, then enjoy the evening.
6. If your shoes hurt, it shows on your face.
7. The only initials one should wear are one's own.
8. Clothes are not life or death.
9. The best accessory… a smile.
10. Rules are made to be broken.

Conclusion

When Audrey Hepburn was asked to share her beauty secrets, her advice was timeless…

"For attractive lips, speak words of kindness.

For lovely eyes, seek out the good in people.

For a slim figure, share your food with the hungry.

For beautiful hair, let a child run his or her fingers through it once a day.

For poise, walk with the knowledge that you never walk alone.

People, even more than things, have to be restored, renewed, revived, reclaimed and redeemed; never throw out anyone. Remember, if you ever need a helping hand, you'll find one at the end of each of your arms.

As you grow older, you will discover that you have two hands, one for helping yourself, the other for helping others.

Illustration by Ross Nugent (1991-2010).

The beauty of a woman is not in the clothes she wears, the figure that she carries, or the way she combs her hair.

The beauty of a woman must be seen from in her eyes, because that is the doorway to her heart, the place where love resides.

The beauty of a woman is not in a facial mode, but the true beauty in a woman is reflected in her soul.

It is the caring that she lovingly gives the passion that she shows.

The beauty of a woman grows with the passing years.

If you share this with another woman, something good will happen – you will boost another woman's self-esteem, and she will know that you care about her."